Dedication

This book is dedicated to my godchildren – Matthew, Michelle, Callum and Jordan – and to all the children whose lives have touched mine in the course of my career. I have learnt far more from them all than I have taught them.

Acknowledgements

My thanks go to those friends and colleagues who have shown a real interest in this autobiography, in particular Dr Shirley Cobbold of the University of Gloucestershire, whose encouragement helped me believe that my story was worth telling. My thanks also go to Cara Le Cureux for her constructive and positive comments, and to Rachel Davis for her sheer enthusiasm.

Finally, I must thank my very dear friends Cynthia and Brian Goodchild for their patience, endurance and support.

To teach is to touch a life forever

Introduction

"THANK YOU FOR COMING to our class," said the little reception class girl as she slipped her hand into mine.

"Wasn't it fun out there?" I replied.

We were walking back into the classroom after I had observed mixed year one and reception class children taking part in a range of exciting and stimulating outdoor activities which their trainee teacher had planned and prepared for them.

There was painting, construction, word building, sand play and role play with toys, all supporting the teacher's objectives of teamwork and cooperative learning. Children were given choices as well as their teacher's expectations of what they would achieve in the lesson. Each group spent time with her turn by turn to learn new sounds and words whilst other groups talked together, mostly peaceably, as they acted out stories or painted pictures. Of course there were the bossy ones, the loud-voiced ones, the shy ones, the organisers and the loners, as well as those who needed a little persuasion to do something new. They were all children with potential to be whatever they chose, and the importance and significance of their teacher's influence on their lives was immeasurable.

It was late March and the weather was windy and the temperature not that warm, but I was once more revelling in the creativity and imagination of a young teacher as she enjoyed her class and developed their learning. How had I come to this delightful and rewarding stage in my own career? Had I ever considered this role of Link Tutor when embarking on my own training for teaching? No. Like many other young students planning to further my education after school, I had simply wanted to become a teacher. Where that would take me was not a consideration or any kind of plan. What transpired has been a lifetime of the unexpected, the joyous, the funny and the challenging. No two days have ever been the same. Children and adults continually surprised and amazed me. The good days far outweighed the bad.

What I have learnt throughout my career I now have the opportunity to share with trainee teachers, whose feelings and emotions about their chosen career will doubtless be very similar to those I experienced as a student. It is a privilege to work with them.

Chapter One
Give Me the Child

WHERE TO BEGIN? WE teach children that every story should have a beginning, a middle and an end, so it would seem wise to start at the beginning. We also teach that every story should have a problem to solve or a challenge to address. There will be plenty of those revealed as my story unfolds!

I was born one Thursday in February 1945, three months before the end of the Second World War, to parents in their mid-thirties who had waited some years for a child. I guess I was what could be described as 'precious' but never really remember feeling like that, as my mother insisted, as I was an only child, that I should not be spoilt. She

Christine as a child

also told me about the rhyme that says, 'Thursday's child has far to go'.

My memories of childhood, like most post-war babies, focus on home-made toys, shopping with ration books and *Listen with Mother* on the radio. We lived in a house in the London suburb of West Hendon, which backed onto the Welsh Harp, a lake across which wires had been strung during the war to prevent enemy aeroplanes from landing. These wires were fixed to concrete bases with iron rings in them. I used to spend hours trying to pull up one of these bases by its ring in order to explore the secret tunnel I was convinced was underneath! My imagination was quite clearly influenced by Enid Blyton's stories of the adventures of the 'Famous Five'. When my father explained what they really were I was very disappointed and immediately lost interest. There was no point in looking for something that wasn't there!

My father worked for 'Pilot Radio' in the war and was due to receive a medal for his part in the work that the company did for the Admiralty. He suffered a duodenal ulcer as a result of his mother's death in the bombings and the pressure of his work, and continued to suffer from it for most of the rest of his life. He was therefore unable to go to the Palace to receive his medal and so it arrived in the post. I remember feeling proud of his achievement but not really understanding what it all meant. I was also upset that he could not meet the King. I remember more the smell of tripe cooking and the revolting sight of the bowl of tripe and milk he had to eat, which I had to carry up to his bedroom. My mother queued for hours to get him fish as an occasional change from tripe, saving her ration allowance each week to do so. These long and rather boring shopping trips came to a welcome end when I started school, and playing shopping with old ration books became a game with more meaning as I learnt to read and count.

I was allowed to start school in the September rather than the January term, which was closest to my fifth birthday. The head teacher had said it would be a shame for me to miss the Christmas activities, so I joined the babies' class. I remember the afternoon naps on a camp bed after lunch each day. I think I must have missed *Listen with Mother*, which had been broadcast around the time of our nap, and have been too awake for my own good. Consequently, I was moved into the middle infant class after just six weeks in school. There I met my first challenge – a formidable teacher! Miss Fairman expected me to keep up with the other children and seemed very cross most of the time. I received a real telling off for leaning too heavily on a blackboard resting on a table, which we stood round to read in turn. My leaning tipped the board up and disrupted the lesson. I was also a trial to her about eating school dinners. The fuss I made resulted in me being taken to personally inspect the food to encourage me to eat. My father's special diet was very low in fat and we all ate the same (except for the tripe!) so I had an aversion to fatty food. School dinners were packed with fat and I just could not eat it. In the end my mother did the mile walk each day to take me home for lunch and back to school in the afternoon. Despite all this, I did learn to read in the middle infant class and had my first experience of knitting.

My top infant teacher, Miss Beecham, was a kinder and

gentler person who helped me to become more confident and self-assured. I took my turn with other children in being her messenger and enjoyed the responsibility. It was on her that I successfully played an April Fool's joke, telling her that she had a ladder in her stocking. I really believed I had caught her out and she went along with it. Now, with a personal understanding of how teachers can 'act', I am not so sure!

In the holidays I sometimes went to stay with an aunt and uncle in Wimbledon who had two sons a few years older than me. Naturally, I had to stand up for myself with these two boys and can recall one of them telling me when I was about six years old that I was bossy enough to be a teacher!

I was very proud of myself when I was asked to perform a dance as a fairy for a special event whilst in the top infant class.

The event took place in the school playground and I had to dance on my own, waving a wand and skipping round to a polka tune. Our next-door neighbours were both concert pianists and their grown-up daughter sometimes looked after me. She had two brothers, the younger the same age as me. I was desperate to practise my dance, so my mother suggested I went next door and asked for some

The dancing fairy!

musical help. Mrs Gunning sat at the piano and played a polka for me and then asked Christopher, my friend and classmate, to play it for me so I could dance round the room to his music. This I did, not realising the significance of his talent. He went on to later arrange music for Dudley Moore and compose music for television and cinema. He received a BAFTA for his music for *Poirot*. I discovered he also wrote the music for the film *When the Whales Came*, which was based on a story set in the Isles of Scilly – but more of that later.

I think I must have been quite an inquisitive child, always asking my parents questions. When their own Victorian upbringing and set opinions made it impossible for them to answer my questions, I simply tried to find out for myself. On discovering a sanitary towel one day I concluded that it was Father Christmas' beard and fitted the loops over my ears and the pad under my chin to demonstrate this to them. They were not amused by my antics and the 'You will find out more when you are older' phrase began to enter their vocabulary. This frustrated me enormously and only made me more curious.

Then there was the dolls' house. My father had taken so much time and care to make it. It had lights with half ping-pong ball lampshades, which lit up, and tiny pieces of real coal in the fireplaces. Sadly, it was not my favourite toy and I rarely played with it. A portent of things to come – I don't have any real enthusiasm for housework!

When I had been at school for a few months I developed acute earache, which was diagnosed as mastoiditis. Developments in the discovery and production of antibiotics made it possible for me to have treatment without an operation. However, this was very new and several doctors visited me at home to assess the situation. They all seemed more interested in my dolls' house than I was and began their time with me by questioning me about it. In my young mind I knew all they really wanted to do was look into my left ear and wished that they would get on with it! I then began to take the medication, which was in tablet form and hard for a frightened five-year-old to swallow. My mother squashed the tablet between folded greaseproof paper and then mixed it with a spoonful of jam. Despite the sweetness of the jam I could still taste the bitterness of the medication. It took many years for me to be able to eat jam off a spoon without anticipating that taste. The infection was beaten by the medication but I had to have my tonsils removed, as this was considered the source of the infection.

Hospital was both puzzling and frightening. Parents were only allowed to visit at certain times and the stress of this made that time tearful rather than joyful. There was an older girl in the ward who had had her tonsils removed and was allowed to walk around, talking to those of us in bed. She was very reassuring and explained some of what would happen after the operation, like eating ice cream! The boy in the next bed was not so calm. He insisted in a very agitated manner that the needle for the injection would go right through my arm. To me that did not make sense. I figured it would be impossible to get the contents of the syringe into my arm if that happened! At that time, *Muffin the Mule* was a string puppet featuring with Annette Mills on the newly invented television.

My parents bought me a Muffin as a present for being good in hospital. It had rings attached to its strings which fitted on small

Muffin the Mule

fingers to create movement. I loved it! A colleague of my father's at 'Pilot Radio' knew how to put more strings on it and attach them to a wooden frame, so my new friend was taken away to be made more complicated for me to operate. Once home, I played with Muffin more than I played with my dolls' house, but did end up spending quite a lot of time untangling the strings!

What I really loved was reading. Every Christmas I could not wait to find amongst my presents a *Rupert* annual. I would sit in bed between my parents, devouring the stories and doing the puzzles. One year when money was particularly tight I also had some knitting needles and wool. That got started straight away as well!

I must have been about seven years old when my father and a work colleague of his decided to start their own business making and selling power units for model railways. This was an up and coming hobby and they caught the market at the right time. As well as trudging to and from my infant school several times each day, my mother also sat in our garden shed in all weathers winding solenoid bobbins on a machine my father had made. Sometimes a neighbour, whose son also attended my school, brought me home when my mother was busy. It was then that I picked may blossom to give to my mother, only to have my gift rejected because it was considered unlucky to have it in the house. This made me feel that I had done something which was very wrong. Despite all my efforts to please her, my mother was always very strict with me. It was my father who played with me and praised me and let me help him with jobs in the home.

The time came when the business needed its own premises and we moved house to Harrow Weald. By then it was the summer term of my first year in the juniors and I became the new girl in a well-established class. The teacher was really kind to me. She certainly didn't throw chalk around the classroom as my previous teacher had done. I joined her Welsh dancing club and the school choir, for which she played the piano.

My second year in the juniors was another encounter with a formidable teacher called Miss Palmer. She was determined that her children would succeed. We had her as our class teacher for three years until we left the school. I realise now that she was preparing us for the Eleven Plus examination from day one, although at the time it seemed like constant hard work broken up only by art, music and craft lessons. I presume we also had some physical education, but it didn't make any great impression on me! I do remember one day having quite a heated discussion with Miss Palmer about the colour of the paint to be used for the trunks of trees on a mural we were painting. She insisted we used the brown powder paint just as it mixed up on its own. I insisted we used other colours mixed together to make the right shade of brown. I don't recall who won the argument, but I do know I felt very strongly about it.

There were some rather naughty boys in the class and Miss Palmer shouted at them frequently enough for me to begin to take it personally. The result was that I decided I didn't want to go to school. I had always loved school and my mother was naturally concerned about me. She spoke to the headmaster, Mr Heslop, who took me aside and explained that the shouting was nothing to do with me and that Miss Palmer was very pleased with my behaviour. I remember feeling very reassured by his words. He was a very tall man and towered over me, but he had a kindly face and a gentle manner. He was the person who, at a parents' evening in my final year at his school, described me as 'academic' in a conversation with my mother and father. When they came home and told me I really did not fully understand what it meant. What I did understand by then was my father's often repeated maxim, 'That and better will do'. For both of them, what I achieved seemed more important than who I was.

I suppose my greatest joy in life was music, and it still is. My family was steeped in Salvation Army music. I was part of the junior choir and my father played in the band and was leader of the Songsters. I sang solos at Salvation Army concerts and at school, where I performed the Gracie Fields song 'At the end of the day' with the choir. Mr Hodges, who then led the choir, once told me that he would love to play for me to sing 'My tiny hand is frozen' from *Madam Butterfly* when I was grown up. That comment boosted my confidence enormously as, believe it or not; I was at times a shy and diffident child. I did learn the piano for a few years, but lessons ended when I passed the Eleven Plus and gained a place at a new girls' grammar school and work had to come first. Amazingly, the free writing task in the Eleven Plus exam was entitled *What I did since I woke up this morning* and it was my birthday that day. Under great pressure, my mother had eventually allowed me to open my presents before I went to school, so I had plenty to write!

There were times when I tried to overcome my shyness. I was taken to a children's party organised by my father's employers at 'Pilot Radio'. We were asked to sing a song or perform a dance. I decided that I would sing, and at first thought I would sing a chorus I had learnt at Sunday school. As other children took their turn, I realised that would not be right for this occasion, so when I stood before the microphone I started singing 'I've got a lovely bunch of coconuts', and to my amazement got to the end without forgetting any of the words and was applauded for my effort!

Hymn practice day was one of the highlights of my week and took place on a Thursday morning straight after assembly. One Wednesday lunchtime, running around the playground, I crashed into another girl. We both went flying! She landed on the back of her head and my nose met the ground. She suffered concussion and I broke my nose. Our parents were notified and my mother took me to the doctor the next morning. He looked at my nose from all angles and thought for a while. He said he thought he could fix it and asked me to sit very still. Then he clicked my nose back into place. I didn't cry but the tears streamed down my face. He told me that I was very brave and said I could go back to school after a few minutes sitting quietly in another room. That was fine by me, as it meant I wouldn't miss much of school hymn practice; and I told him so!

Living on the outskirts of London in a vastly expanding urban area and visiting relatives in Wembley and Harlesden, my life was very much town centred. Even in Harrow Weald, the local 'rec' was just a play space for ball games with a few swings. I went there with friends and spent most of my time 'working up' as high as I could on a swing to see the boys over the hedge in the next field playing football. There were a few bushes and trees in the 'rec', but it was not what could be described as the countryside. Then in February 1956, for my birthday, some close friends of my parents, whom I came to know as Auntie Muriel and Uncle Derek, gave me a book called *Jane's Country Year* by Malcom Saville. This was a story I could not put down. It told of a girl who had been very ill and was recovering with relatives in the country. It described all she learnt about the natural world, plants, animals and life on a farm, and how she shared this with her family in the letters she sent them. Suddenly, my horizons widened and an interest in nature that later became a passion for science was ignited. I often wonder where my interests would have focussed had I not read that book. It was timely, too, as I began seven very happy years at Heriots Wood Grammar School the following September.

Chapter Two
The Teenage Years 1956–1963

FOR ME THERE WAS nothing more exciting at that time than being part of a brand new school. There was one year ahead of my intake which had started the school in some old school buildings in the locality with the deputy head, a Mrs Shucksmith. The new building was ready when my year group joined and the head teacher, Miss Williams, took on her role. The grounds were not complete and so a friendly site manager was still occupying his little hut situated part way up the main path to the school. His cheerful greetings made a good start to the day and kept us informed of progress on our playing fields and tennis courts. When all was complete, he and his hut disappeared.

There were only three of us from my junior school who moved to Heriots Wood and I was not particularly friendly with either of them, so I had to make new friends. I got to know most of the girls in my class, which, in the first year, was mixed ability. After the tests that year we were put into three streamed classes and I just made the top class. It was then that firmer friendships began to develop. The work was challenging but I enjoyed it enormously, except for French. Miss Ergis and I did not get on and so my progress in French was not great. My parents were no linguists so I had no help at all until a new French teacher, Miss Rochat, arrived in the fifth form. Her more flamboyant and enthusiastic manner captivated me and suddenly I got a far better grasp of French, just in time to prepare me for the O level exam. I was no great shakes at PE either and found netball too rough and hockey just too much running. But then came dance, where body movements could interpret music and I found my niche.

One year, a group of us were asked to perform a dance for an Open Day. We had to dress as Greek maidens and appear from the woods behind the school to perform our dance barefoot on the lawn, music pouring from a classroom window. Isadora Duncan had nothing on us! The short white tunic I made for the dance was later transformed into a tennis dress, as I was slightly better at tennis than netball and hockey. There were many special moments when I found that dance gave me the opportunity to express emotions hitherto suppressed by my upbringing. Even now when listening to Saint-Saëns' 'Danse Macabre', in my mind I am back in the school gymnasium moving expressively to the music. In the sixth form we were given choices about our options in PE and naturally I chose dance. It helped me get through the tough times in the A level course when the end seemed to be ever farther away and some relaxation was badly needed.

The O level biology course was interesting but not well managed, as the teacher had no real control of the class. Miss Foster was not comfortable teaching large classes. As I know from personal experience, teaching the lesson on sex education is guaranteed to get the full attention of the class. Her analogy of squeezing toothpaste from a tube with the sex act caused great hilarity amongst a group of highly charged hormonal fourth formers. Our good manners, and possible disciplinary action, ensured we contained ourselves until after the lesson!

I suppose I could be described as a somewhat serious 'goody-goody' at school. However, that wasn't always the case; mostly I didn't get caught. One day three of us were chatting in the girls' toilets when we should have gone outside for break. One girl sat on the edge of a washbasin, which we were told emphatically never to do, and I commented, "What if old Shucko comes in now?"

A voice from the door said, "She's here!" and Mrs Shucksmith appeared. We made a hasty exit!

As well as my interest in music I also loved drama. Playing a part was sometimes far more engaging than being myself. I volunteered for school plays and went along to auditions. My first important role was that of the hind legs of a horse. As one of the characters had to jump on and off my bent back during the performance, all I really gained from that experience was a sore pelvis. However, things did get better! In our English lessons we were studying Shakespeare's plays and I was entranced with his stories and his language. The school play was to be *The Taming of the Shrew*, and to my delight I secured the part of Baptista, the shrew's father. Busty girls in Shakespearean costumes playing men's parts and wearing false beards required some imagination on the part of the audience, but they managed it.

A parent who worked in the make-up department at The

Old Vic theatre in London offered his services and transformed us into our characters with his skills. The smell of almonds will always remind me of the grease paint, the nervous tummy and the excitement. My Baptista beard was a great improvement on my Father Christmas beard!

Baptista

We were not allowed to take part in school plays in our O and A level years, so the lower sixth was my last chance for a part. One girl, Pat Newell, and I had always been rivals for important roles. With hindsight it is easy to say that the teachers chose the best girls for each role, but it did not feel like that when she pipped me to the post each time. I lobbied Miss Creek, the school play producer. I had read Falstaff in our O level lessons for *Henry IV, Part One*, and loved the character. I wanted to play him and thought *The Merry Wives of Windsor* would be just the right play for the school production. Pat could play one of the wives and we would both be happy! Miss Creek did not agree and would not be persuaded. Instead we were to put on two short plays – *Everyman* and Brect's *The Caucasian Chalk Circle*. I got to understudy the lead in *Everyman* and play Shauva the village policeman in *The Caucasian Chalk Circle*.

That kept me too busy to bother Miss Creek again.

At my birth my mother was told I had an adult nose. It is my finest feature and the only part of me which is long and thin. I got called 'Roman nose' at my junior school and had to learn how to cope with the name-calling. I felt very hurt. All girls together can be pretty beastly, too, and at one stage some of my so-called friends at Heriots Wood chanted, "You're a horrible hag and we hate you," as I walked down the path out of school. Once more I had to cope with that myself. Bullying was never mentioned in school, and as I thought it was sure to be my own fault, I did not mention it at home. I tried to find out what I had done to incur their wrath, but was told it was a joke – some joke! It couldn't have been long after that that I persuaded my dad to let me ride to school on my bike. That avoided the long walk down the path and meant he did not need to give me a lift to school any more. I had bought the bike myself out of my earnings from working at his factory on Saturday mornings. Although the business was doing well he was insistent I learnt about the value of money and the importance of 'saving for a rainy day'. I had to work for what I wanted.

My mock O level exam results in Latin and geography were not good and so I gave up those subjects in order to concentrate all my efforts on the other seven I was taking. That meant I no longer needed to wake early in the mornings to try to learn the Gallic Wars for Latin, and I guess Miss Trollope the Latin teacher was relieved, too. However, I was doing well in my favourite biology, physics and chemistry lessons and really enjoyed English, even getting to grips with most of the clause analysis. Needlework was a joy and mathematics was all falling into place. My acting talent came in handy in French, particularly in the oral exam.

At the end of every school year we had to copy the school reports our teachers had written into a special book designed for that purpose. It was a tedious and much-hated task for most of us, as it gave us time to think about what our teachers considered to be our strengths and weaknesses. One year my form teacher made a comment which inferred I learnt by rote and not by understanding what I was taught. I was most affronted by this and genuinely upset that she thought this of me. I had always made a real effort to understand even the subjects I found most difficult. However, it did spur me into ensuring I really did understand my work and that she noticed I did.

I was, of course, a member of the school choir and we were part of the annual concerts, which included instrumental items. My father was eager to hear the choir but did not hold back on his comments about the violin classes' contributions. I guess he would have preferred brass to 'scrapers', but even brass can be discordant when children start to learn. He assured me our singing made up for the pain of the violins.

At about this time I was entered for a public speaking competition organised nationally by the Salvation Army. I was an active member of the Corps Cadets, a young people's group in the Army which focusses on Bible study and discussion in preparation for possibly becoming an officer. I preached the sermon one Sunday morning at a Corps Cadet weekend when I was about fifteen or sixteen. Entering the public speaking competition was simply an extension of this activity, or so I thought. I had to write my own speech and perform it at local and then divisional venues. There was one other girl at our corps who attended a grammar school. We had both passed the Eleven Plus examination, which consisted of English, mathematics and verbal reasoning tests, while our other friends had not and consequently attended secondary modern schools. This resulted in us both being teased by the others who called us names like 'grammar grubs', but at least in that situation we had each other's support. That changed when it came to the competition where we became arch-rivals. We both got through the local heats of the competition, but she won and I came second at the divisional level. Being second best was becoming quite familiar to me.

Teaching each week in Sunday school from the age of thirteen came naturally to me. I knew my vocation was to teach and that to be able to get to university or teachers' training college I had to work hard at school and pass both my O and A level examinations. That became my focus, possibly to the detriment of my social life outside school. I passed all seven of my O level exams, even French! We had to prepare postcards for our head teacher to send us our results. It was far more personal, and easier to read, than the computer printouts we got for our A level results. Miss Williams wrote a comment: 'Well done, Christine!' It meant so much to me. Then came the big decision – which subjects to choose for my A levels. My main interest was science, but I also loved English. We had been guided into choosing either arts or sciences, so I chose science. However, Mrs Riddle, the physics teacher, had told me quite categorically that my maths was not good enough to do physics. Mrs Green, the chemistry teacher, had told me she would have me in chemistry, but did not think I would pass the exam. That, of course, made me more than ever determined to do so. The solution to all this depended on a telephone call to Miss Williams. I decided I wanted to take botany, zoology and chemistry. She agreed. Whilst her staff may have had some reservations about me, she believed I could do it and that faith in me was all I needed.

There were two of us taking botany, seven taking zoology and twelve taking chemistry. How lucky we were to have such low numbers, but then it was the early 1960s and there was a focus on education that must have meant more money had come into schools, possibly a result of the 1944 Education Act and delayed somewhat by the post-war stringencies. Miss Foster was totally different when teaching just the two of us botany. She was a brilliant teacher. We spent the whole of the lower sixth working with plants and microscopes, identifying cell structures and functions and doing some ecology work in the local area. She also sent us to Slapton Ley field study centre in Devon on a week's course. We began to worry about when we were ever going to do some theory work. That came in the upper sixth and, due to the skills we had learnt the previous year, fell easily into place. Chemistry was a struggle for me, particularly the organic chemistry, but spending Saturday evenings away from the television and working through all my notes and textbooks helped me achieve some degree of understanding of it all. But the practical came naturally to me. I enjoyed the challenge of analysing an unknown substance using procedures we had been taught and of carefully measuring quantities of liquids needed to form new substances. I even got the calculations included in these practi-

Christine Hammant

cal tests right, so my maths was not that bad after all! Zoology was based on the dissection of a range of invertebrate and vertebrate animals, which was fascinating, but the smell of formaldehyde did linger on the hands however much one washed them afterwards!

In addition to our main subject studies we also had 'general studies', which covered a range of topics long passed from memory. However, one notable session was with the local vicar who came in to talk about relationships and told us, to our horror, that an engagement to be married could and sometimes should be broken. His viewpoint was the subject of many a discussion amongst most of us for whom love and

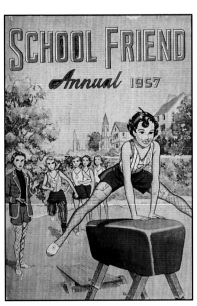

School Friend Annual, 1957

marriage was a starry-eyed goal in the future. His influence was very different from what we read in magazines like *Girl, School Friend* and *Girls' Crystal,* where every love story had a happy ending.

It was not long after we all left school that we heard that his marriage had ended, and his words came back to haunt us.

The only A level practical examination we took in school

was chemistry. We felt safe in the familiar surroundings of our own laboratory and for me the exam went really well. I identified my substance and completed the calculations in the time allowed. I achieved an 'A' grade for the practical. For the botany and zoology practicals we had to go to London to university laboratories. Travelling up to London from Stanmore was not difficult. A group of us had been going to The Old Vic regularly throughout our sixth form years to see plays, usually twice a term. My role in the first few years at Heriots Wood as the savings monitor had developed into that of theatre trip organiser in the sixth form, and we knew the route into London well. Going to a strange laboratory with other students from different schools was not so easy. I was very nervous. In the zoology exam we got the very dissection I had hoped we would not have – dogfish. However, the botany was better. My place at Portsmouth College of Education was dependent on me passing all three A levels. I just hoped I had done enough to achieve that. Despite his famous maxim, my father positively encouraged me to go to training college rather than university because he did not want me to struggle with work that was too hard for me. At that time it was probably the best choice, but I do confess to feeling rather aggrieved about it.

I was on holiday in Wales with my parents and a friend from school when the A level results came in the post. We were staying in the hotel part of the complex where there was also a campsite. My results came with the morning post and were brought to our breakfast table. My friend's were not. Enquiries revealed that her post was with the campers' mail, and when we had found her letter we opened them together. We had both passed all our subjects and my place at teacher training college was secured. Spirits were high and we were both eager to find out how our other friends had fared.

So the time had come for us all to pursue our various careers, some to universities, some to polytechnics and some to teacher training colleges. We left a school, which by this time had become established as one of the best girls' grammar schools in the area, and we had been a part of creating that image and setting its traditions and ethos. I for one was very proud of that. Our final assembly was very memorable in several ways. First, it was the only end of year assembly that one of our friends actually got to attend. She missed all the others as she was usually crying in the girls' toilets. We ensured that she did not miss this one. Secondly, the head teacher had decided to read out the names of all 'her' girls and where they were to next go to further their education. It was the time of the Profumo affair. One girl's name was Christine Keeling, but Miss Williams read it as Christine Keeler and the assembled company dissolved into laughter. The somewhat tense atmosphere of a farewell assembly was broken and we all relaxed.

Early in the lower sixth I had applied to the City of Portsmouth College of Education and, following an interview with the Principal, Mrs Jean Williams, was offered a place for September 1963. Passing from the care of one Williams to another seemed like a good sign. I liked the place and felt that I could be happy there.

Chapter Three
College Days 1963–1966

THIS WAS THE SUMMER holiday with no work for examinations! I did have a reading list for college, though, and read avidly *The Shrimp and the Anemone* by L.P. Hartley. It was a story about children, and provided me with insight I would not otherwise have had about how children play and think. It made a great impression on me; one I feel may be worth sharing with prospective trainee teachers. That year my parents had moved house to Watford, as the business had expanded and a new and larger

Working on the factory 'line'

factory was required. I worked full time in the factory to save for the books and PE kit we had to have for college. The boring monotony of the work, either on the 'line' testing the finished products or in the packing department preparing goods for dispatch, was only relieved by listening to the banter of the other workers.

These were the women who could be the mothers of children I may one day teach, and it was interesting to learn how they thought. It was fun sometimes to let slip some harmless information about the 'boss'!

I had asked for a car of my own for my eighteenth birthday, but instead received a large box inside which was another box, and another, and another until I found a model Austin Seven Mini. I felt so disappointed that it was hard to take the joke. I was, however, promised a car for my twenty-first birthday, but the wait seemed interminable. The journey to and from Portsmouth continued to be by train. On the way home one summer term I decided to travel back from the mainline station on the Metropolitan line to Watford Met station, as it was just a walk across a park to where we lived.

The station was the end of the line and so the carriages gradually emptied of people as we got nearer to my destination. There was just one man left in my carriage and he came and sat opposite me. All my senses were telling me there was something wrong. I did not look at him or speak to him, but he spoke to me. He said, "You have a nice kind face." I did not reply but looked out of the carriage window. As we approached my station, I moved nearer to the carriage door, and as soon as it opened I rushed onto the platform. He left the train as well, but I did not look to see where he was going. I knew there was a phone box outside the station and went straight there to call my father to come and collect me. I then went into the little shop nearby and waited for my father to arrive. It was such a relief when I saw his car draw into the station forecourt and I ran and climbed in it. Never again would I travel home on that train!

I did eventually become the proud owner of a pale blue Austin A35 during the Easter vacation of my second year at college. After a couple of unsuccessful lessons with my father at home, I signed up for lessons in Portsmouth, where I took my test and failed! More lessons with one of the staff at my father's factory and a friend from the Baptist church my parents were then attending got me through the test in time to take the car back to Portsmouth for my final year.

At the start of year three, my zoology lecturer and personal tutor Harry Pascoe commented that he thought that I was at last really enjoying college life. He also suggested to me that I might consider embarking on an external degree course at a London University College in my first few years of teaching. This advice quite amazed me, as I had resigned myself to the qualification of a 'certified teacher' rather than that of a graduate. Suddenly, my horizons seemed wider than I had imagined possible. In the event, that did not happen quite as soon as he had suggested, but it did eventually and was an education degree rather than a zoology degree.

There was an operatic society at college, which, of course, I joined. I relished the excitement of rehearsals and performances each year and even had a love song written for me to sing in my final year production. The student lyricist was dashing and handsome and I found myself just a little bit in love as I sang the words he had written just for me! I joined the Madrigal Society and the college choir and was able to have singing lessons. Part of the deal was to have piano lessons as well, and that was a struggle, but the lecturer who taught me was very patient and this prepared me to take and pass grade five theory of music, which I needed to be able to take my grade six singing exam.

One year the members of the Madrigal Society decided to climb onto the flat roof of the great hall to sing a motet for Ascension Day. Promptly at 6.30 a.m. we climbed the fire escape ladder, music in hand, and sang. It was wonderful: a sunny summer morning and beautiful music floating across the campus. Later that day one of the girls in the hall of residence nearby told me that she thought she had died and gone to heaven and we were the angels singing!

To my delight there was a drama department in college, and in my first year this offered a speech and drama course which all students had to attend. I found this really invigorating, as we always ended the lecture with a relaxation session where many of us fell asleep. As part of the course we had to produce a presentation on a theme. My group was given 'Maturity' and it fell to me to find the material for this. I enjoyed this research very much and we presented a super interpretation of what we considered maturity to encompass. It was great fun rehearsing and performing our presentation.

The department put on one major production each year and in my first year this was *A Midsummer Night's Dream*. I auditioned and two of us got the part of Hermia, which we performed on alternate nights. It was performed in the round, which was quite an innovation at that time. However, it did have its draw-backs. As the warden of our hall of residence put it, "I prefer to see my fairies as light and ethereal, not hear them thumping down the aisle beside me!"

The following year a main drama course was introduced and the course students, naturally, took on the main parts in produc-tions while we plebs stepped aside.

Lectures in most subjects were good. The science depart-ment was headed by Dr Ashby, a keen ecologist, whose recently published book on the subject featured quite often in his lectures. We students joked about his frequent references to the lawn-mower as the 'mechanical cow' and its influence on plant growth and survival, but what he taught us certainly made its mark on my teaching. Another trip to Slapton Ley was part of the course, where I discovered quadrats and line transects, which would later be used both in school fields and on the Isles of Scilly.

The English department was on the ball and the new lecturer demanded a great deal of reading and book reviewing, skills of analysis destined to later serve me well. However, not so the mathematics lecturer, who waxed eloquent on the extensive use of Cuisinaire rods, a colour-coded maths resource, ad nauseam. I was glad I had such a sound basis in mathematics O level when it came to teaching the subject. I found the art, craft and lettering lectures a real outlet for my developing creativity, and my skills in lettering have been well used ever since. Our PE lectures were hilarious! Moving 'feet leading' over a bench or mat was a new experience for me. What was even more amusing was watching the mature students, ex-RAF personnel for example, trying to do likewise and maintaining control of their giggles! The education lectures were varied with outside speakers on occasions, but the seminars were very informative.

When outside speakers were invited to address lectures to the whole year group, students were expected to give the vote of thanks at the end. I had managed to avoid eye contact with the student responsible for organising this for a while, but eventually the day came when I was asked to speak on behalf of all present. Listening to the lecture, knowing that I would have to draw out some points from it to mention at the end, kept me fully focussed. My words of thanks couched in the context of the lecture were warmly received by the student body, and I was much relieved. That was another experience I could add to my collection, which would be of considerable value in the future.

My first teaching practice was at a village school on the Isle of Wight. A group of students had been allocated places at schools on the island and we stayed at a small hotel from

My First Class

What I Did Since I Woke Up This Morning

Monday to Friday of the four weeks we were there. Whilst the other students went back to college at the weekends, I stayed on the island at a hotel owned by an aunt and uncle in Sandown. Naturally, I was well looked after and spent some happy times with them and my cousin, experiencing a freedom in family life I had not known before. The school was a joy. I taught a class of eighteen eight- to eleven-year-old children in an old Victorian building, where a kindly headmaster gave me good advice and much encouragement.

There was a large field very close to the school where we discovered a variety of flora and fauna in our science lessons. Doc Ashby would have been very proud of me. I only had one visit from a supervisor, who watched an RE lesson and spotted a spelling mistake on the board. It was from her I learnt the ruse of asking the class if they could spot the deliberate mistake I had made! This practice quite simply served to confirm my conviction that teaching was definitely the career for me.

As I was on a junior/secondary course, my second teaching practice was at a secondary school in Gosport. Getting to the school each day was an experience. The student union minibus took those of us travelling to Gosport down to the harbour to catch the ferry. Once on the other side of the harbour we had to catch a bus to the school, carrying all our files and resources needed each day. This meant our start was early and our day was long. However, the school provided many useful and interesting opportunities for developing teaching skills. My supervisor was on this occasion a science specialist and his support and guidance firmed up my specialist knowledge and understanding. We were on the same wavelength and I really enjoyed this practice.

Then came the big decision. I had to decide whether my final placement should be in a primary or a secondary school. I chose secondary. My reasons were twofold. First, I felt it would give me the chance to teach my specialist subject and use the skills I had in it to enthuse young people. Secondly, I felt a kinship with older children and wanted to support them as they developed into adults. I did not feel it was right for a teacher to have favourites and was concerned that this might happen if I taught very young children. So I was placed in a girls' secondary modern school in Southsea, where mostly dock workers lived. These girls were tough and outspoken. One day I was having trouble getting one particular girl to settle to her work. It was sports day and she was expected to win most if not all her races. She was playing with a tennis ball in the lesson and I asked her to give it to me. She refused and I told her that she would not take part in the sports day if she did not hand it over. She said, "You can't do that; you're only a student!"

I replied, "Oh yes I can." She handed over the tennis ball and reluctantly got on with her work. Bluff is a very useful skill sometimes!

Feedback on the work we did in college was minimal and our progress was not shared with us. It was, therefore, an enormous surprise to learn that due to a new lecturer discussing the exam questions with her seminar group before the final papers were taken, we would be judged on continuous assessment. For those who had not revised much for the exams it was a great relief. I had worked hard to prepare for them and felt somewhat cheated, but the feeling soon wore off. However, when the final results came out I had gained credits in education and curriculum subjects and achieved the advanced level in biology.

I had taken my Salvation Army uniform to college with me and attended the Southsea Corps on Sunday mornings on a fairly regular basis. I went with a friend to the local parish church in the evening. I was nothing but ecumenical! Our Assembly Choir led a wonderful Advent carol service in the church each year and there were concerts by the music department. It was my task to sing 'I know that my redeemer liveth' when we performed extracts from the *Messiah*. Singing with an orchestra was a new experience for me and quite overwhelming, especially as I had only just emerged from sickbay after a dose of gastric flu and laryngitis. The lecturer who conducted the orchestra gave me almost continuous eye-to-eye contact as I sang, encouraging me and helping me to hold my nerve. It was a very special moment.

Chapter Four
Beginning a Career 1966–1970

ALL TOO SOON IT was time to go home, as I had promised my parents I would, and find a job. I was offered a job after an interview at the local area education office. Two of us had left Portsmouth and returned to Watford, both science trained, and there were two secondary schools on a particular estate needing science teachers. As mine was a junior/secondary course and Anne had taken a secondary science course, we had not met very often at college. Now we were both facing similar challenges. The estate had been built to rehouse families from London slums twenty years previously, and there were some very challenging characters in the school to which I was sent. Imagine a young, still somewhat naïve biology teacher facing a class of rebellious fourth-year leavers. I asked the senior teacher what the discipline in the school was and was told, "You make your own." So I did! It was tough, but I liked the youngsters, showed them respect and believed in them. Yes, lessons were noisy, but work was completed and some young people even wanted to talk with me after lessons and in the playground.

What I Did Since I Woke Up This Morning

There was one girl in my tutor group who suffered from petit mal, which is a mild form of epilepsy. Those who suffer from it present as vacant and not aware of what is happening around them. This was not something we had been taught about at college and the first time she had an 'absence' in one of my lessons it took me completely by surprise. I had no idea what to do. Not so her friends, one of whom said to me, "It's okay Ma'm; Roberta's gone again; she'll be back in a minute." Sure enough, within a few seconds Roberta had regained her consciousness and just had to sit quietly for a few minutes and have a drink of water. I learnt quickly how to deal with this situation and checked that other staff knew about it.

Next door to my biology laboratory there was an art room equipped for pottery work. The teacher there decided to start an evening class for would-be potters and I joined. It was great fun messing around with clay after a day in the classroom. I still have my one 'masterpiece', which acts as a very reliable door-stop! At the time I needed the 'therapy' this activity offered, as it was becoming increasingly difficult to live at home after the freedom of college life and I was looking for accommodation of my own. I found a bedsit which seemed suitable and was making arrangements to move there when my parents decided to buy me a small terraced house and start me on the house ownership road. They retired to Hampshire at about the same time.

The deputy head of the school, Mary Salter, was a rather special lady who took the girls for a 'Good Grooming' course she had developed and published as a book. At the end of my first year of teaching, the school closed and combined with the other secondary school on the estate to create a new school.

Mary moved on to teach at the local college of further education. She told me if she could have taken another member of staff with her to the college it would have been me. What a compliment from such an experienced teacher.

The new school was bigger and more impersonal. Skills I had learnt from my head of department in my first year came in very useful, like driving the school minibus and making use of audio-visual equipment in my lessons. I had a tutor group to register and mentor as well as my teaching role, and I was part of a house system. Life was very busy. I had followed up my singing lessons at college by enrolling at the Watford School of Music and was preparing for my grade eight exam, but pressure of work made it impossible for me to take it. I was disappointed but knew it was the right decision. Maybe sometime in the future I would be able to focus on it again. In the meantime, there was the fun of sending my naughtiest boy and his classmates from my laboratory into the music room next door and hearing them sing, or try to!

In my first year my friend from college and I had run a combined field study course for our pupils at a Youth Hostel Association study centre in Portsmouth. It had been a really worthwhile experience and so I decided to repeat it over the next two years, but at different locations. We stayed at Charlbury in Oxfordshire on one occasion, and as well as doing some excellent woodland ecology involving, naturally, the by now famous quadrats, we came upon a village celebration one Sunday afternoon and joined in the fun. It included a strawberries and cream tea, which went down very well with the girls, especially after youth hostel food. Accommodation in youth hostels was very much the same wherever we went. It comprised separate dormitories for males and females, usually with bunk beds and adults and children all together. Sometimes we were the only occupants of the dormitory and so, in true Joyce Grenfell style, I would wish the girls goodnight and turn out the lights, hopeful of an uneventful and peaceful night's sleep. That was not what they had planned. I am told on good authority that as soon as I was asleep the high jinks began. Consequently, I was the person wide awake and ready to get going the next morning while the girls were rather less energetic.

Our stay in Blaxenhall, Suffolk, where seashore and grassland ecology was the focus, also had a night to remember. There was a poster in the youth hostel announcing that a group was to appear at a local pub. I was asked by the girls if they could go along and I agreed, but followed on behind them only to discover that the 'group' was middle-aged and played the washboard and spoons! They were no match for the Beatles! The weather on this trip was particularly good and the girls were eager to improve their suntans. As we were busy investigating the seashore life we noticed a smell rather like that of a fish and chip shop. It appeared to be coming from one of our number, who admitted to having a home-made suntan lotion which was a mixture of oil and vinegar. It might have done something for her suntan, but it did nothing for her popularity!

The town council parks department contacted my school for some students to work, with a teacher, on a conservation project in a local park. The biology teacher was the obvious choice for this project, especially with her keen interest in ecology. So I accepted the challenge and asked for volunteers. A group of about eight fifth-form girls, who had all finished their exams, plus a friend of mine and I set off to the park one sunny Monday morning in July to find out what we had to do. The park ranger explained that we had to clear thickly growing waterweeds and algae from part of the stream which ran through the park. These plants were blocking the flow of the stream and it needed to be freed. We were dressed in shorts and tee shirts so a little paddle was no problem. That was until we realised that the bed of the stream was stony and slippery and the water contained leeches, which rather liked to latch on to our skin. The plants were pretty firmly embedded in the stream and tough to pull out of it. It was hard work but great fun. We chatted, we sang, we moaned, we got suntanned and we got very hungry. We all stank of the stagnant stream water and at the end of each day we washed ourselves off in a cleaner part of the stream before climbing into the school minibus for the drive back to the girls' various homes. By the end of the week we had accomplished our task and duly reported on our activities in a subsequent assembly.

The music teacher, whose room was next to my laboratory, was a very gifted musician. In addition to teaching and training young musicians in the school, he also directed musical productions. He decided we should perform *The Mikado* at the end of the autumn term one year. It was to be a combined staff and student production. I was invited to take the part of Yum-Yum and had two sixth-formers as my other two 'maids'. The male lead, Nanki-Poo, was the RE teacher and our kissing duet caused quite a stir amongst the pupils! It was a time of great enjoyment both in rehearsal and performance. The school orchestra played for the show and once more I found myself singing solo to orchestral accompaniment. It was an incredible experience. The backstage team was amazing, especially with their imaginative use of props for the encores of 'Here's a how-di-do'. My parents planned to come up to Watford to see the show, but sadly my father had a mild heart attack and they could not make it.

One of the 'three little maids' left the school to move to Cornwall shortly after *The Mikado*, as her father had secured a job in the Liskard area. She was extremely upset at leaving and I popped round to her house to check that she was okay at lunchtime on the day she was leaving, exceeding my responsibility as her teacher. I was late back to my laboratory and found not only my class waiting for me but the deputy head as well. I learnt a salutary lesson that day. However, this was the one student who kept in touch with me throughout my career and became a personal friend.

In my fourth year in secondary education I began to realise that I might be better suited to teaching younger children. Middle schools were being introduced in various parts of the country and in Berkhamsted a newly appointed head teacher called Colin Kefford was overseeing the building of a brand new middle school and advertising for staff. I applied for a position at the school and was appointed. This was the start of an extraordinary and inspiring phase in my career.

Chapter Five
The Augustus Smith School
1970–1978

HOW MANY TEACHERS, I wonder, have been both a member of
a new school themselves as a student and then taught in a new
school? I guess I might be one of a privileged few. September
1970 was the beginning of the rest of my life in so many ways. I
had a new home and the freedom to come and go as I pleased, and
a new job where I could help to create the standards in learning
demanded by an innovative and highly motivated head teacher.
Colin Kefford gathered around him staff with a wide range
of talents and the energy and drive to keep up with his initiatives. The school was named after a man who had been born in
Berkhamsted and who became the Member of Parliament for
Truro. Colin had researched the history of Augustus Smith and
discovered that he had appointed himself the Lord Protector of
the Isles of Scilly and started education on the islands. We opened
the school with 270 eleven-year-olds in the September, and by the
following June they had all visited the islands, camping on the

main island, St Mary's. This was to become an annual residential school trip for several years, initially under canvas and then later in accommodation on an off-island called Bryher.

My first visit to Scilly in 1971 was enough for me to return to my friends and their two young children in Watford and describe with such enthusiasm the beauty and peace of the islands that they were prepared to help on a work camp on Bryher the following year. The day we arrived the tide was so low that we were landed on a shingle outcrop with our luggage and given vague directions to find the schoolhouse where we were to stay. The school secretary's husband and two parents of pupils in the school were with us. We managed to fit in some sightseeing and complete the redecoration tasks needed in the school building, which was a few minutes' walk from the house. We determined to come again to this wonderful part of the world, and have done so for over thirty years, bringing family and friends with us to share in its peace and tranquillity. We are, to put it frankly, addicted to the place. We have made good friends of fellow campers on the campsite on Bryher and have shared barbeques in sun and rain and still returned for more.

Staffing a trip to the Scillies was a challenge; after all, we did have to leave enough teachers, admin staff and cooks behind to run the school. Parents and governors were invited to join the trips and did not need much persuading. A parent, another teacher and I were the advance party one year. We arrived on site at St Mary's a day or so before the children and began erecting the large tents used as marquees. It had been an early start and a long trip, and we suddenly realised that we were very hungry. As we had left the school, one of the support staff had given me a tin filled with home-made date slices. This was the time to open the tin and tuck into them. Nothing could possibly have tasted so good.

There was healthy rivalry between each group of children and staff as they set off to visit different islands: which group could complete the walk around the island in the fastest time, or who could spot the greatest variety of birds or plants. My group had extra equipment, the quadrats. These were used to sample particular areas of land for the dominant plant, while a line transect provided an estimate of the most frequent plants along a given distance. This was particularly interesting on areas like sandbars where seawater invaded at high tide. The children learnt the history of the islands on their walks as they discovered Roman settlements and Anglo-Saxon burial chambers and visited the museum. They spent time sketching dramatic rock formations created over millions of years by earth movements and the weathering influence of the wind, sea and rain. They got suntanned and in some cases sunburnt. Calamine lotion was an essential part of the first aid equipment. Most important of all, they learnt to live as a community together and have fun. Each group was different and character traits unseen in school came to light. The homesick got comforted and the noisy got quietened. My cooking skills had good practice with advice from the cooking staff we took on the trips. One day I laboriously chopped up all the cabbage for the evening meal for over a hundred children and adults. It took hours. The cook returned from her day out with the children to tell me that it had not been necessary; the cabbage would chop down as it cooked! Many years later I happened to meet an ex-pupil of Augustus Smith School working at a leisure centre. Her most vivid memory of her time at the school was the visit to the Isles of Scilly.

Colin Kefford had initially appointed me as the teacher with responsibility for natural sciences, and I was to work with the head of science. The school covered the age range of nine to thirteen years and operated more on secondary school lines than primary. The curriculum changed almost annually as we tried out Colin's latest ideas. One of these was to introduce a session when children could choose activities from a selection offered by staff. I offered a craft session where children could learn crochet and macramé. One child gave me a challenge I could not refuse. She wanted to learn to crochet but she was left-handed. She could not follow my right-handed demonstration. There was only one solution. I had to teach myself to crochet left-handed and then teach her. I spent considerable time at home transferring the process to my left hand and managed to perfect it. The girl in question then had no problem following my demonstration and learnt to crochet very well.

Colin also changed staff responsibilities on a fairly frequent basis and I moved on to become girls' counsellor, head of year and senior woman teacher. His commitment to the school was unquestioning. The children picked up this notion from his enthusiasm and admired his determination to always do more for the school than he asked them to do. He raised money for the school by doing a twenty-four-hour sponsored walk around the perimeter of the school over a weekend. He was in school as usual on the Monday, but he was wearing his slippers to soothe his blistered and bleeding feet. One of my class wrote a story, which I showed him. It described the school building collapsed, bricks and rubble everywhere, with him in the middle of it all rebuilding it as fast as he could. It was not surprising that when he gave each child ten pence to use as in the parable of the talents to raise funds for charity the response was amazing.

Once embarked upon teaching with training observations behind us, few lessons were formally assessed or reviewed for most teachers in the 1970s. Not so those of us at Augustus Smith School. Colin came round lessons quite often and talked to the children about what they were learning. In one of these lessons I had shown the children how to measure the capacity of their lungs using an inverted bell jar, a large bowl and a length of rubber tubing. They were busily doing this when he came into the room and asked them what they were learning. His smile told me that he was very happy with the replies he got. Naturally, he gave us verbal feedback on his professional assessment of our work, which, in my case, enabled me to further develop my skills of teaching and class management.

I was teaching a class one day around the time that the comedian Dick Emery was very popular on television. The class was proving difficult to settle at the start of the lesson. In exasperation I exclaimed, "Oh, you are awful!" and the response came back in unison, "But we like you!" We all laughed, relaxed and everyone got down to work straight away.

I was sometimes asked to lead worship in our assemblies and was very happy to do so. At the time we had a very talented guitarist as the music teacher and I asked him if he knew the song I wanted to use in the worship. He didn't but was able to accompany me once I had sung it through to him a couple of times. It was based on the story of the Samaritan woman who met Jesus at the well, and required the children to shout out a one-word question in parts of the song. The story and the song went really well and one of the newer, younger members of staff commented afterwards to me, "Chris, you have real charisma."

Colin supported any member of staff who wanted to develop further professional skills, and as a consequence I attended a year-round gardening course. In one day at the authority's conference centre, which had amazing grounds and gardens, we learnt and practised the gardening best suited to that month of the year. My personal knowledge of the annual cycle of growth in a garden improved no end and I was able to pass this on to the members of the gardening club at school. Included in the school building was a greenhouse, which was thereafter well used. Jamie Oliver would have been very proud of our efforts!

I also studied for a further qualification in field studies. This was a much more academic course and included laboratory work, lectures and fieldwork. We had to complete a year-long project of our own choice to demonstrate the skills and understanding we had acquired. I went back to the nature reserve area of our local park. This time I was identifying and counting freshwater snails on a regular basis in order to identify the influence different conditions had on their population and numbers. My data formed the basis of the report I wrote on the project. Going down to the park in the summer and autumn was easy, but I had to force myself to face the winter visits to my 'spot' in the nature reserve. To my relief, I gained a pass for the course and the project. It was in one of the laboratories at Hatfield Polytechnic, where the course was held, that I spotted a wall display which read, 'Have you thanked a green plant today?' It gave me great food for thought and I have used the question on several occasions as a theme for harvest thanksgiving services in school.

One of Colin's fund-raising ideas was to hold a Continental Week in the school, where each night from Monday to Thursday we had meals from various European countries served in the hall, with entertainment, to parents, governors and friends of the school. The cookery teacher planned the menus and the children cooked the meals. The music teacher organised and rehearsed the entertainment, which featured the music of the country whose food was being served. I had just sung in the chorus of a production of *Kiss Me Kate* by a local amateur operatic society. This show is set in Venice and as our first evening was 'Italy', I opened the entertainment with a rendering of 'Another opening, another show' while the audience was served pizza and pasta. The children then took over for the rest of the week. It all went so well that some parents came twice.

It was while I was at Augustus Smith School that I realised that not only could I make costumes for various productions, but also props like bonnets and banners. I learnt how to do macramé from an American Dominican nun called Sister Janet. She came to England on a teacher exchange and needed somewhere to stay. One of the members of the Baptist Church that I attended was the deputy head of the school where

she was to work as a teacher. He was having difficulty find-
ing accommodation for her and asked me if I would consider
having her to stay with me. I am so glad I said yes, as she
became a good friend and was patient enough to teach me
macramé. We shared many happy times talking school and
spending time with friends of mine and their two children,
who came to know her as 'Aunty Jat'. She introduced me to
the inspiring book *Jonathon Livingston Seagull*, which I was
to later use in my teaching. She has returned to England since
that year for special family events and we have visited her and
her family in Wisconsin. She has set up an Eco-Justice centre
there, which includes an educational element where groups of
students come to learn about honouring and conserving the
natural environment.

After four very happy years, crammed with a multitude of
experiences, at Augustus Smith School, I decided it was time
to move on and applied for a Primary School deputy headship. I
did not get the deputy headship at the school but was offered the
position of head of juniors, which I accepted. The school had just
had a major fire in one classroom and when I arrived the head
teacher was engrossed in the rebuilding project. The deputy
head who had been appointed went on long-term sick leave
and I was asked to become the acting deputy head. I also had a
year five class of thirty-eight pupils. The head teacher needed
me to be a sounding board for his concerns about the building
and this often encroached into lesson time. Consequently, my
class suffered and he was critical of my teaching. Things were
not going at all well and I was very unhappy and disillusioned
by his autocratic attitude to me. Due to the fire, one class was

decamped each term to some old school buildings a coach ride away and I was very relieved when it was the turn of my class. Now I was able to give them the attention they deserved and create the purposeful learning environment they needed. I read the story of *Jonathon Livingston Seagull* to them and was able to use this to further their spiritual development. I realised how popular a book called *The Lion, the Witch and the Wardrobe* was amongst my pupils and read it for the first time myself. That was a spiritual experience for me. However, I had decided to leave the school and was able to return to Augustus Smith for a further three years before I was appointed as the woman deputy head at a middle school in Borehamwood.

Chapter Six
Becoming a Deputy Head Teacher 1979–1985

IN MY LAST YEAR at Augustus Smith School I had begun an in-service Batchelor of Education degree course at a local college of higher education. I decided to study the philosophy of education and child development as my two major options, with health education and educational technology as my minor options. I enjoyed the challenge of the two major options very much, but it was in health education that I received my only 'A' grade for an essay, which was planning a scheme of work to teach sex education. As part of our educational technology course we were asked to produce a cine film, as there were no video cameras in general circulation in the early 1980s. I decided to film the range of vegetation on Bryher, where my friends and I regularly camped in the summer, and used their daughter as a comparator of plant heights across the island. I cannot recall the grade I received for the work but I know she and I had a great time making the film. The course required one day release per week from school plus two evening sessions for the lectures and seminars. Fortunately, my new head teacher was happy to honour this commitment and I embarked on a new stage in my career whilst furthering my professional development.

There were two deputy head teachers at Holmshill, one male and one female. The male deputy's responsibilities included arranging cover for absent staff and writing the timetable, plus overall pastoral care for the boys. The female deputy had to deal with pupil absences in liaison with the area education welfare officer and pastoral care for the girls. We both had teaching commitments in addition to these responsibilities. The male deputy head and I did not interpret 'pastoral care' in quite the same way. He tended to make extensive use of the power of his position and of detentions, while I tried to get alongside the girls, understand their situations and reason with them. His strategy was a 'quick fix', while mine took more time, energy and patience. After a while at the school I began to realise that he was aiming to undermine and discredit me. This was particularly the case when I asked the head teacher to broaden my experience and allow me to write the timetable and sort out cover for absent colleagues. This he did, and it did not go down too well with my 'other half'! It was not too long after that that he secured a headship and a new male deputy was appointed. We worked quite well together most of the time, although I could not honestly describe it as a rapport. This time I was the established deputy and female and he found that hard to accept. He was one of those people whose jokes just never quite worked so that there was always that awkward silence at the end!

One of the staff at the school was quite outspoken about me

being 'too understanding' with our pupils and made this clear to me. I was, therefore, very surprised when he later came to me and said that he had been attending a church and become a committed Christian and wanted to tell me that he could now see what I was trying to do and admired me for it. Apart from thanking him for what he said I could not think of anything else to say, as I was so astounded. From then on I had his full support and cooperation.

My main subject teaching was again science and I worked in a rather old-style laboratory with long benches, each served with a gas supply. I had the support of a laboratory technician who had worked in the school for many years and had a high regard for the science teacher I was replacing. He had been very keen on rural science and just outside the laboratory there was a rural studies area composed of a large greenhouse and a small patch of land fenced in with chain-link fencing. This was cared for by a rural studies assistant. On my arrival I soon spotted the chicken feathers on the mat in the lab where my predecessor had plucked chickens reared in the rural studies area, and also the hops growing on the chain-link fence. This could be very interesting, I thought!

My lab technician was very knowledgeable in science and felt that it was her role to check that I was likewise! On one particular occasion she was quizzing me, and when I had provided the correct answers I challenged her about her attitude. From then on we got along fine. There was just one problem. She smoked. Usually this was just before school and in break time in the prep room with the windows open and the lab doors closed. At that time it was not a political issue. Then one morning before school

I went over to the laboratory to leave a note for her to find that somehow an individual had got into the lab, which was locked, and turned on all the gas taps. If Doreen had lit a cigarette when she arrived, it could have been disastrous. I turned off the gas, opened all the windows and left her another note. Working with Doreen was my first experience of having another adult in my classroom who contributed to the learning atmosphere. It was great being able to banter with her about the improvement in a child's work or the behaviour of the class. She was even enthusiastic about the two gerbils I decided to keep in the laboratory. When they arrived I asked the children to suggest names for them and we had a vote for the final decision. What or who influenced the outcome I cannot say, but the gerbils were named Gin and Tonic!

As a deputy head, my role was to deputise for the head teacher whenever necessary. My 'other half' did not like taking assemblies, but this was not a problem for me. Sometimes I just had enough time to find a story and pick a hymn when the head was called out and I had to cover. Other times I was able to plan in more detail. On one occasion I decided, as children were becoming very self-centred, to focus on being selfless with a little reverse psychology. I engaged the help of the music teacher and sang 'All I want is a room somewhere' from *My Fair Lady* and then asked the children what the song was really about. We eventually got to the point!

It was at this school that I had my first encounter with child abuse and drug abuse. I had taught about drugs at Augustus Smith School but had never come across it for real. Then one day there was a new boy in my class. He was rather dozy and unable to attend fully. He was thin and looked neglected and he had dribbles of glue down the front of his rather worn and tatty jumper. The head teacher knew about him and was in contact with social services. He did not stay at the school for long so I did not really get to know him, but I felt very sad and shocked that a child should be in a situation like this. On another occasion I saw the head teacher examining the bruises on the face of a boy. He told me later that he had immediately called in social services to address the issue with the parent. Previously, I had not had to deal with girls fighting, just boys, but at this school the first incident referred to me was a fight between two girls which had resulted in one of them having her pierced earholes torn and they were bleeding. I spent a great deal of my time working with children whose understanding and respect for others was sadly lacking. It concerned me enormously and I was searching for an opportunity to address this issue in a constructive and positive way when one presented itself to me.

It was a warm summer afternoon and sports day had just finished. The children were sauntering slowly back into school, tired and cheerful after a pleasant afternoon of mostly friendly and fair competition. Some parents had joined us and they were beginning to leave for home or were waiting for their offspring. As I watched from the door of my classroom I saw Mrs Peters striding purposefully in my direction. 'What can she want?' I thought to myself. I had not had much to do with her as with some parents in my role as deputy head. Her son was not a problem as far as I knew, in fact quite the reverse; a pretty reliable chap from all I had heard.

"I have an idea to put to you," she said once the pleasantries had been completed.

"I'm intrigued," I replied.

"Well, I have recently started a new job at a local home for mentally and physically handicapped children. I am the welfare assistant working with the teacher and I was wondering if the school would like to link up with the home in some way."

This was the beginning of a most amazing experience for the school and for me. I decided to start an after school club where children would visit the home one afternoon a week and help in any way we could. I plugged the idea in assembly, put up a notice for children to sign and waited. The response was good. Enough children wanted to join to make the club workable and a rota of visits was set up. We all soon got to know the children at the home as individuals. There was Tommy, who could just about say hello and smiled all the time, and Bhumi, who fiercely defended her right to be independent, sometimes scratching but other times grinning. There were the babies, who stayed just a short while but were a joy to feed and help to bathe. Each of the children was strapped into a wheelchair and unable to communicate in any way but their own. Gradually over the weeks, we came to know their personal characteristics and to see the very small steps that they made in their learning and celebrated with them.

Then came the day when the sister in charge at the home asked me if we could put on the nativity. How could we possibly achieve this, I wondered? But the challenge was too much to resist. My children understood the needs of their special children and could cope with any mishaps which might occur. It only remained for a script, scenery and costumes to be created.

The nursing staff dealt with the costumes, I wrote the script and persuaded the woodwork teacher to provide the one piece of scenery we needed. My children learnt their words and where and when they should move their character in his or her wheelchair. Finally, rehearsals were over and the big day arrived. The school hall was packed. The minibus with our Mary, Joseph, shepherds, kings and angel had arrived, ready in their costumes. The show could begin.

The script was short and the action minimal, but the impact was tremendous. I have never witnessed the nativity story where the atmosphere was so electric and the audience so enraptured. Nothing went wrong: no child fitted or moaned, no one forgot their lines. It was perfect, just as Christmas should be. I know how this whole experience influenced my club members, as I heard their comments in the playground, rebuking children who disparaged disabled people. I hoped our special nativity story had influenced others in the school to be more understanding and respectful of each other.

Being responsible for attendance in a school where children and parents did not always see school as important was a challenge. As I got to know the children, so I knew who would inform on others who might be truanting. Checking the registers regularly gave me a clear picture of who the regular offenders were and whether they had genuine reasons for being out of school. Therefore, armed with all the information I could gather, I went round to homes on our estate and retrieved children who should have been at school. Attendance began to improve. Liaising with the education welfare officer was a vital part of this strategy, as she had information from other sources which addressed our concerns.

During the first two years of my deputy headship I completed my in-service degree and was awarded my BEd. I decided to continue for one further year to achieve the honours award. I was required to pursue some educational research and write up a report. I decided to test, teach and re-test one of my classes on Piaget's theory of conservation of matter. Another class was also given the tests but not the teaching and used as a control group. Part of the teaching for this was some ecology work in a conservation area in the school grounds, which involved, yet again, using the quadrats. These were my own personal property, as my father had made them for me in my very first year of teaching, and so they went with me wherever I was working. For the uninitiated, a quadrat is simply a wire frame a quarter of a meter square which is thrown randomly on the ground and the plants in that area are identified, recorded and counted.

By this time I had worked in Hertfordshire teaching science for nearly fifteen years and attended courses run by the science advisor. My degree work had been successfully completed when my head teacher had a visit from him requesting that I should be released to trial some science practical testing with eleven-year-olds. The Government had set up an Assessment of Performance Unit and it was this body's brief to assess the viability of testing children's ability to carry out practical scientific problem-solving tasks. My head teacher agreed to release me for half a term for this work. There were a few days' training in London and then, equipped with my car boot full of apparatus, I set out for schools in various areas of London. The tasks were designed to be used with one child at a time and so schools were asked to select pupils from a cross section of ability and gender. The tasks were interesting and gave me ideas for my own teaching, which I later used. The children were generally quite confident and tackled the tasks with interest, although I did have one girl who completely froze and did nothing at all, and I asked her teacher to take her back to her class. For some children, working one-to-one with a stranger could be daunting. The testing was extremely time consuming and labour intensive, so it was not surprising that it was never introduced into schools.

In addition to my science teaching I also taught a few classes social studies combined with religious education. I felt strongly that these children needed to develop their listening skills, so at one stage I read them *The Lion, the Witch and the Wardrobe* in my lessons. They were entranced. The dance and drama teacher heard about this from them in her lessons and must have picked up their enthusiasm for the story. She decided to make this the next school production. We initially planned together and I wrote the script for the first part of the story while she created the dance into which the story developed and directed the drama. The costumes were a challenge, but we had an older member of staff who seemed able to conjure up everything that was needed from her vast stock of colourful garments accrued over many years. It was a tradition in the school that her year group, who were the youngest children, would perform a nativity play each year. I was in their shared area when she was allocating parts. She knew the names of the children in her class, but not the other two classes and therefore had to ask some children to tell her their names. One child did not know what to answer. He looked at his teacher and said, "What name shall I say?" I shuddered to think what experiences he had had to bring him to this point in his young life.

The very enthusiastic head of English at the school decided that the staff should put on an improvised version of *A Midsummer Night's Dream* using non-Shakespeare language. We discussed the plot and decided how we would perform the story as an improvisation. There were rehearsals but they generally ended in hilarity, as we anticipated the children's reaction to what we had planned for them. I was cast as Titania and squeezed into a friend's wedding dress for my costume. If I said anything coherent in my role it was a miracle, as the whole event was so funny that I was stifling laughter all the way through. We enjoyed ourselves and the children had a ball.

One of the highlights of my time as a deputy was a canal boat trip. A year group leader called Dave had organised a trip which comprised one boys' boat and one girls' boat for an October half-term holiday. He was in charge of the boys' boat and another female staff member and her husband were able to supervise the girls' boat for the first half of the week. I was asked to take over when they left. I talked to a friend, Cynthia, and she agreed to come if we could take her daughter with us. It was all arranged and as we waved goodbye to my colleague and her husband, so began four very eventful and hilarious days on the canals. To start with, I had never been on a canal boat before and did not have a clue about steering it. Cynthia, fortunately, took to it like a duck to water. We followed behind the boys' boat as instructed, but they managed to get well ahead of us. I'm not sure if that was due to the power of their engine or to the fact that we liked to chat with other travellers on canal boats! It could have been due to one or two individuals falling in the water 'accidentally on purpose', or the occasional stop at a hostelry for refreshments. Nevertheless, we ended up, after taking a wrong fork in the canal, late one afternoon at a rather quiet spot which felt a little 'spooky', and realised we needed to turn around to begin our return journey. The boat would not turn in the space we had. What could we do? Just then, another boat came along and two strong and very helpful men bounced our boat round and we were able to search for a better place to moor for the night. The girls had to shine their torches along the canal bank for Cynthia to see clearly in the moonlight to steer us to a safe mooring! When we eventually caught up with the boys' boat, the teacher in charge appeared surprised to see us. I actually wondered if he had intentionally led us astray by giving us the vague instructions which resulted in us taking that wrong fork in the canal. Thanks to our own ingenuity and a little help, we were able to deflate somewhat his feelings of male supremacy!

Our school was situated very near the shopping centre in Borehamwood and some of the older children went out at lunch times to buy snacks or pop home for lunch. Often this was an excuse to see if they could spot any famous TV actors who might be working at the nearby studios. *Eastenders* was filmed there. They certainly had more success at that than I did when I went shopping after school. It was after one of these lunchtime sorties that the head teacher was contacted by the police. A pupil had been seen shoplifting in a chemist's shop and identified by her uniform but not apprehended. From the description we were able to narrow down the culprit to one of three or four girls. By clever questioning, the head teacher identified the miscreant. He asked me to search her desk while he questioned her. What I found was a veritable hoard of 'trinkets', all of which could be bought at the shop in question. She was taken to the shop to return them and apologise, and her parents were informed.

The local Teachers' Centre in Borehamwood kept astride of the developments in education which were beginning in government in the 1980s. I attended courses and contributed to working parties to write locally agreed science syllabi and supplementary papers for the agreed syllabus in religious education. Then a course entitled 'Curriculum in Action' was run, and my participation in it gave me the credibility I needed to apply for a place on a Masters Degree Course at The Institute of Education in London University. My head teacher came to me with an offer of a year's secondment to take the course and I enthusiastically accepted his offer. After nineteen years in the classroom I now became a student again and was once more travelling by train. My previous experience on a train taught me to always get into a carriage where there was another woman.

Chapter Seven
University at Last! 1985/6

MY PARENTS HAD ATTENDED my BEd honours degree ceremony and were proud of my achievement. Only my mother knew I was able to gain a higher qualification as my father had died in 1985 before I had secured my place on the masters' course. I often wished he had known about my year at the Institute, if only to prove to him that his fears about my ability to cope with degree level study had been totally unfounded.

I had sold my two-bedroom terraced house and moved to a bungalow nearer to my friends whilst at Augustus Smith School. After much considered discussion a few years later, we all decided to move in together so that I would have company and we could all benefit from a larger house and garden. By this time my godchildren were into their teenage years and needed the extra space and an aunt nearby to talk to sometimes. Help with homework was an added attraction. The support of my 'family' was essential as I studied and researched for my MA.

We all followed the major curriculum module, which with hindsight it is clear was preparing us for the onset of The National

Curriculum. We were taught by lecturers who had themselves written books, which, naturally, they recommended us to read. As a minor module I took gender studies, which was a select group mostly of women, where we thrashed out feminist issues and looked at the place of women in history. Education seminars were interesting, as each student had to lead one in turn. I recall I began my seminar by giving the group a task to complete while I sang a Nana Mouskouri song to them which would assist in the task. Was I mad or just prepared to make a fool of myself in order to achieve the objective I had been set? If I wanted to become a head teacher then the latter had to be the case!

I met some very interesting people on the course. One of them was a senior education administrator in Australia. As I got to know her I felt able to ask about teaching salaries in Australia, which rumour said were much higher than our salaries. She was unable to answer my question. It had been a condition of her getting a place on the course that she did not reveal that particular information. With that I had to be content. However, she did accept an invitation to come to my friends' silver wedding anniversary celebrations during that year, as did our American nun friend. It was quite an international event.

A central part of the degree course was the research we had to complete and write up as a thesis. I decided to research reading across the curriculum. I had an instinctive feeling that middle schools would not survive as a permanent part of the education system in all areas of the country and I wanted to be ready to move into primary education. The key to that, for me, was a better understanding of the process of learning to read and how this was implemented in schools. I contacted infant schools and infant departments of primary schools in my local area and went along to observe lessons and talk with teachers and head teachers. Everyone was very helpful and I collected data which proved most valuable in writing my thesis. It had to be printed and then professionally bound, and despite several checks before taking it for binding there is still one spelling error on the first page! What is it that is said about reading what you want to see and not what is written?

I applied for several primary school headships during the latter part of the course and obtained one interview. It was for a headship in Edgware and would mean I would move out of Hertfordshire to the London Borough of Barnet. If I did not secure this position I would return to Borehamwood. My future was in the balance. I had an interview one evening at Barnet Town Hall. I wore a yellow linen suit I had made and slipped a fur jacket over my shoulders. I sat at a table while my interviewers were seated at other tables in a U-shape in front of me. The questions are a blur, but the comment from the chair of governors of the school after I was appointed will stay with me forever: "You are lucky to get this job. I hope you will make a good go of it."

His tone was rather terse and it deflated my exhilaration somewhat, but not for long. In fact, it made me more determined than ever to prove to him I could do the job and do it well. I visited my previous head teacher in Borehamwood to tell him my news. For some reason he had not been asked for a reference so the news was a complete surprise. His verbal congratulations were followed by a lovely letter thanking me for all I had contributed to the school in wisdom, good counsel and subject planning.

My new job started in early September 1986 and our MA

examinations were two days before that. The summer 'holiday' was spent revising for two one-question papers, chosen from a selection offered, in a three-hour time frame. Focussing on the new job had to be on hold until the exams were over.

It was sad to say goodbye to people with whom I had shared a new and exciting time in my professional development. We exchanged addresses and kept in touch for some years. I still receive a Christmas card from my colleague in Australia and we exchange news of our families and work. It was not until November that year that I received the news that I had obtained my MA qualification.

The degree ceremony was at The Albert Hall in London and Princess Anne conferred our degrees. My very dear friends Cynthia and Brian, who had shared in the ups and downs of the

course, came along to see the ceremony, and then we went out for a meal that evening to celebrate with my goddaughter and her nanna, who had become like a surrogate mum to me. My godson had started a history degree course at Nottingham University that term and was the only member of the family missing from the celebrations.

M.A. (Ed)

Chapter Eight
My First Headship at a Junior School 1986–1993

THE FIRST TIME I walked up the drive of the school was on a visit there a few days before the interview. It was an April day, the sun was shining and the cherry blossom on the trees bordering the playing field was in full bloom. It was such a beautiful sight and one I was to enjoy for eight eventful years. I was greeted warmly by the school secretary and met the retiring head teacher, who took me on a tour of the building and gave me background information on most of the staff. The feeder infant school was located very nearby and I was told that the infants came to the junior school for lunch, helping to create a familiarity which aided smooth transition from one school to the next. The school was built just before the Second World War had started and on a tight budget. Provision was very basic. There were additional classrooms outside the main building, some of which had been in use since the 1950s. Despite the inadequacies of the building, such as no toilet facilities in the additional classrooms, there was a positive, friendly and busy atmosphere, and the retiring head spoke of the many happy memories he would have of the school.

The deputy head teacher had also applied for the position and having met her on my visit I recognised her at the interview. She had taught for several years at the school where she had met and married her husband. They were both still teaching at the school when I took over the headship. The school is located in a mixed housing estate, and in 1986 the intake was predominantly from Jewish families with some Indian and Chinese children, who all mixed well with the indigenous British population. It was a truly multicultural community. The secretary lived on the estate and knew many of the families and was able to provide very valuable background information when it was needed.

Newly appointed head teachers had to learn on the job in the 1980s. There were no qualifications required to become a head teacher other than having previously been a deputy head. It was assumed that this would provide the necessary skills, which was a very sweeping assumption. Fortunately, schools in Barnet were allocated local authority advisors who visited new head teachers quite often in their first year and could always be contacted by telephone. My advisor gave me a really crucial piece of advice which served me well. He said that if I felt something needed addressing, I should 'make a nuisance' of myself to get the problem solved. So that's what I did. I had learnt from Colin Kefford at Augustus Smith School that one had to make dreams happen and that it involved hard work and commitment. He showed me that a good school uses the talents of its staff to the very best advantage and that adults as well as children respond to praise, encouragement and challenge. As a deputy I had learnt to fight for my rights and earn the respect of my colleagues and to believe in what I was doing. I knew by the time I arrived at my own school that change for a purpose was far better than change for change's sake. So where should I begin?

I took a long, hard look at the school to assess what was being achieved and what the next steps forward should be. Most classrooms were furnished with very old and out of date paired, iron-framed wooden desks with a bench seat and sloping desktop reminiscent of those in the 1950s. These had to go and be replaced with colourful tables with removable drawers located underneath. I negotiated with the local authority furniture department and new tables were duly ordered and delivered. The cost far exceeded the 'new head teacher' grant I had been given, but the authority managed to find the money. The music teacher had no classroom of his own and neither did the special needs teacher. There were relatively large spaces in the building which could be converted into teaching areas for these subjects. More 'making a nuisance' resulted in these changes being implemented. The school had a flat roof which was beginning to leak. When it rained, buckets were needed in certain parts of the corridors and classrooms. After many telephone calls and letters, repairs were done, but these were never totally successful. Finally, the day came when the building was completely re-roofed, but not until we had waited for the previous contract on the roof to end. I have always believed that learning can progress best in a welcoming and comfortable environment and that staff feel valued if their working conditions are regarded as important. Improving the standard of the building and furniture was, therefore, my first priority.

By 1988 the Education Act was in place, which would implement the National Curriculum. Schools received information about this and a file for each subject, which subject coordinators were expected to work through with their colleagues to create the school's own programme of study. We joked about needing a wheelbarrow to carry around all the files we had been given! Whilst my teachers were wrestling with this insurmountable workload, for which we were given minimal support, I was beginning a journey called 'Local Management of Schools'. I attended many seminars with other head teachers to learn about the devolving of money to schools and how we should manage our own budgets.

The previous head teacher had initiated some fund-raising activities in order to leave a substantial amount of money for me in the school fund, the school's own bank account which was used as a working account for uniform sales, trips and activities like swimming. I managed this account, which had to be audited annually. Setting out the account in the appropriate way took me back to my mathematics lessons at primary school. Now I understood why Miss Palmer had made us add columns of figures both across and down the page and aim to get the same answer both ways. The only difference was that then the calculations were in pounds, shillings and pence. My deputy, who was the mathematics coordinator and had a good knowledge of accounting systems, helped the secretary manage the school budget when funds were devolved to schools. The system we devised worked well and I was asked to share this at meetings with other head teachers. However, the school did not have enough funds in either of these accounts to purchase, in the first instance, the computers which were needed in every classroom and so some serious fund-raising had to start. I learnt that a Parent Teacher Association had existed in the past, been successful for a while, but then closed. I re-opened it as 'The Friends' and by my first Christmas at the school we had the first of many very successful Christmas fetes. There was one partic-ular parent whose enthusiasm drove this event and who cajoled others into getting involved. She told me in true Jewish fashion, as she dashed off to buy items for her stall, "Chris, you have to spend money to make money!" She was right.

I have never been one to expect from others what I am not prepared to do myself, and so twenty dozen home-made mince pies and other cakes were my contribution to the cake stall. I painted a large banner announcing the fete, which was tied to our front fence for a week beforehand for our neighbours and passers-by on foot, in cars or on buses to see. The first one I made was stolen, so the next year I made another, which, this time, the school caretaker checked on each night. For the children the main attraction to the fete was Father Christmas. They all knew that it was our senior male teacher in a costume borrowed from the infant school, but of course, they enjoyed the fun of it and perpetuated the magic for their younger siblings. My deputy's husband dressed as an elf and collected the money as children visited 'Santa's Grotto'.

Each year we had a television personality to open the fete and then sell autographs. My special needs teacher had contacts with actors in *Eastenders*, as her husband was an accountant for many of them. She asked them to come to help the school at no charge and provided a meal that evening for them in her own home as a thank you. It was a really good arrangement. Ross Kemp, one of these TV stars, was very charming and interested in the school when he came. At Holmshill I had worked with Jennie Barnet's mother, and one year I was able, through her, to ask Jennie to open the fete. I had not actually taught Jennie at the school, as she had left just a year before I began working there. At that time she was a popular TV personality and, like Ross Kemp, easily recognised by pupils and parents. The fetes, and other fund-raising events, allowed us to enhance the quality of the education we offered the families in our area, as even with local management of schools, funding for education was barely sufficient. These events were hard work and great fun and cemented positive relationships with parents and friends of the school.

Attention Deficit Hyperactive Disorder was beginning to be recognised in the 1980s and 1990s and the drug Ritalin was prescribed by doctors to enable children to concentrate for longer and learn better. A child was transferred from another local school to us suffering from this condition and was prescribed the drug. In addition, an art therapist was employed by the authority to work with him at our school. As I saw the benefits of both medication and therapy on his behaviour and on his ability to concentrate in class, and his mother told us of the improvement at home, I realised that we could help other children in this way. This was certainly the case with regard to the art therapy, for which I had other candidates ready and waiting, and so the wheels were set in motion. Once a week, two or three children benefitted from 'time out' with the art therapist and were able to draw and paint as they talked through their difficulties. Playtimes were generally calmer, lessons less frequently interrupted and the whole school saw the changes in certain individuals.

When I arrived at the school there were staff eager to share information with me which they felt would be helpful. The music teacher, who had been at the school some years and was comfortable in his specialist role, gave me some very useful tips regarding what aspects of worship would encompass all the religions represented in the school. He advised me to avoid the name 'Jesus', so I used 'Lord' instead, and to always ask the children to stand for prayer. This worked very well. He took hymn practice and taught the children a wide range of hymns and songs. When he did his annual 'Top Ten' hymns, it was 'A New Commandment' which came out as number one. This utterly Christian song had captivated the Jews and Muslims as well.

The literacy coordinator, a very intelligent and highly emotive Jewish lady, was keen to tell me about the school 'shows'. She made it quite plain that the school became a drama school twice a year, at Christmas and in the summer, when musical shows, like *Oliver*, were performed. I decided to wait and see what happened the first Christmas. It was amazing! The music teacher taught the songs in his lesson prior to the auditions for parts and then rehearsals began in earnest. The children learnt stagecraft as well as acting. They learnt about teamwork and about the importance of focus and concentration. Every child in the school was involved. It was a well-oiled machine which purred into action with all staff roles allocated. I was 'front of house', advertising and selling tickets. Each performance was to a hall full of families, friends, governors and older siblings expecting an evening of high quality entertainment, and getting it. Of course, I had concerns about the justification in educational terms for the lesson time spent in rehearsal, but then I looked at the enthusiasm and vitality the shows generated and at the data I was gathering on pupil progress and could find no concrete evidence that the shows were inhibiting progress. As the National Curriculum gradually put greater pressure on staff time and the expectations of the children, it became necessary to limit the shows to one a year in the summer; but the sparkle they created never died. It was a joy to be working in my office and hear the singing in the hall as they rehearsed.

Mother Goose

The children were not the only people in the school who could 'perform'. The literacy/drama teacher persuaded the staff to perform pantomimes, which she had written, to the children. She had a rather more inhibited cast to deal with this time, but of course, she managed to create a fun experience for both performers and audience. No expense was spared. We hired costumes, we learnt lines and we practised songs. I recall performances of *Cinderella* and *Mother Goose* in particular. As head teacher I was cast in the leading role each time. The performance of *Cinderella* was going well until I forgot to leave my slipper behind as I fled from the ball. What could I do? I just took off the shoe and threw it the length of the hall just missing a child in the front row. It added to the excitement and put a new slant on the story!

Liaison with the infant school was something I was keen to strengthen. The head teacher's name was Sharpe, and one governor frequently quoted 'Sharpe by name and sharp by nature' to me when speaking of her. I did not find this to be the case. Yes, she 'boxed for her corner', but then so did any head teacher with the learning, social and emotional needs of their pupils as their greatest concern. She worked hard to ensure every child left her school able to read, understand numbers and know how to behave. She understood about the importance of learning through play and that children who needed it should have support in their learning. My school benefitted enormously from the wonderful start the children had in their early years of education. Before I arrived, the two schools had run quite independently of each other, although they had a joint governing body. I wanted to change this. My staff needed to see how children were taught in the infants to understand how to take this learning on further in the most effective ways. So began a slow but effective process of liaison and exchange visits with one very special outcome. At the suggestion of the infant school head, we agreed to produce a joint school brochure, which had a tuck flap in the back cover where details of each school could be added. It was a major project which drew the schools together and was probably one of the first 'glossy' school brochures with colour photographs produced in the area. We were very proud of it indeed.

The school celebrated its fiftieth birthday while I was there.

This was another joint event with the infant school. I had researched the history of the school from archive material and produced a document outlining important events over the fifty years. Included in this were the details of the former head teachers of the two schools, which proved useful when we decided to provide benches for the children in the junior playground. On each bench were the name and dates of one of these head teachers. They became quite a talking point for the children. There was a very talented dance teacher on my staff who was involved in producing and directing amateur dance and drama with adults. Inspired by an idea from a television advertisement, I talked to her about using the children to create a picture of the name of the school as part of our birthday celebrations. She took on board my idea and planned dance movements to music which all the children could learn and then each class would end the dance in

Broadfields glossy school brochure

the position of their letter in the word. First she taught the dance routine to the staff, and that was the real challenge! We had such fun trying to achieve what the children found quite easy to do. On the day of the performance we all walked over to the infant school where the event was to take place. In the grounds there was a sloping bank with a flat grassed area at its base. This was perfect for the dance routine. Some governors and parents joined us and the dance began. Each class had different coloured scarves to hold to make their letter shape clear. I took some photographs, but oh how I wished I had been able to magic a helicopter to get a real bird's-eye view of the performance and film it.

The school had previously used the swimming pool on site, but when I took over the role of head teacher it was no longer in use and in a bad state of disrepair. I did research the possibility of repairing and improving this wonderful additional facility in the school both for the use of the pupils and the local community. Sadly, the cost of this was completely out of our league and I was unable to raise any sponsors to support us. I was so disappointed that I was unable to make this particular dream a reality. On the other hand, I did instigate occasional fun days for the pupils, where special activities took place outdoors in which all could take part; and there were weekly sessions where staff offered a range of activities which children could choose, such as learning French, enhancing football skills, painting, drama, singing and mathematics games. Children's achievements were acknowledged and rewarded and a special 'Courtesy' badge awarded each week to the child in each year group who had been well mannered, polite, helpful and respectful to others.

The head teacher of the infant school informed the governors that she would be retiring from headship when she gave her report to a governors' meeting. The previous item had been some discussion about the branch of Barclays Bank which had been set up in the juniors, and this had interested one of the rather elderly and hearing impaired governors. The resignation of the infant head was an important item, but he missed it and interrupted to ask a question about the bank which was totally irrelevant at this point. He had no idea what he had done and there was considerable coughing to cover laughing in the room. Fortunately, the infant head teacher just smiled and did not take offence. It was a moment to be remembered.

The importance of support staff in any school should not be disregarded. At my school we had a conscientious caretaker, his assistant and cleaners, who were appointed by the authority, and canteen staff under the direction of the cook in charge. The school was clean and the meals were nutritious. Welfare support in classrooms was only in relation to children with statements of special educational needs. I envied the infant school the extra general classroom support they had. Our assistant caretaker was very helpful to staff with any repairs to classroom equipment which might be needed, and for this they were most grateful to him. Sadly, I came to the opinion that he was not the person he purported to be.

I had attended a course on child abuse and learnt about the characteristics of paedophiles. I passed on the course materials to my deputy to read so that she was also informed. I was out of school one Friday afternoon prior to attending a training course related to school management at the weekend. That afternoon my deputy had a visit from a parent of a child in year three who had told her mother that the assistant caretaker had been abusing her. My deputy did not believe her and told her this kind of thing could not happen at our school. She had clearly not read the information I had given her. Despite being advised by my deputy not to go to the police, the mother sensibly did so. There followed over a year of police investigations and waiting for a court hearing.

Even though there was evidence from several children of sexual abuse, my staff could not accept that this kind and helpful man had behaved in this way. They were asked not to question the girls involved, but some of them did. I was called to court to give evidence relating to the layout of the school building. My deputy was called to give the accused a character reference. The children were interviewed on closed circuit cameras and the chief educational psychologist for the Borough sat with them and stopped the interrogation when it became too much for them. The school educational psychologist supported me, as I was the only member of the school staff who actually believed the children, and visited me often at school. My family, amongst whom was a trained counsellor, and my church were an incredible support and this made it possible for me to be in school every day.

A parent of one of the children came into school one afternoon straight from the court. She was very distressed and wanted to talk. She told me that she had had to leave the proceedings to dash to the toilets to vomit when she heard the evidence from the police doctor confirming that her daughter, aged eight, was, as she described it, no longer a virgin. I felt sickened at what she told me and could only listen and offer her my understanding and support. I could not turn back the clock.

On the day that the verdict came from the court and I was informed that the accused was 'not guilty' it was playtime and the staff were all in the staffroom. I took a deep breath and went in to tell them. There were a few comments made about it being the right verdict, which I ignored. I left the room to get my coffee and return and as I picked up my coffee mug I heard the cheer coming from the staffroom. This made me extremely angry. I took another deep breath and went in to tell them that I would be arranging a training session for all staff on child abuse in the very near future. This followed a few weeks later.

The chair of governors came to see me shortly after the abuse case was closed. He had done his homework. He told me that the assistant caretaker could, as he was found not guilty, return to work at the school. I told the chairman, "If he comes in the door I will walk out."

A job was found elsewhere for him and I now had to rebuild my relationship with the staff who had so bitterly disappointed me. I addressed the issue with my deputy in her appraisal interview later that year when I felt calmer and more rational and she had had time to think about what she had done. The school slowly got back to normal, but the five children involved in the case did not return. They were found places in other local schools by the chief educational psychologist, who knew that they would no longer thrive with us. Their parents thanked me for my belief in them and their children and I have a lovely card from the children, which I treasure. In it they thanked me for believing what had happened to them was true. One parent told me, "You are the best thing that has ever happened to this school."

What I Did Since I Woke Up This Morning

Disappointment can be overcome by forgiveness and we had a job to do educating other children. We got on with it and gradually over the two remaining years that I was head teacher at the school, relationships reached an amicable equilibrium. In fact, I still see some of the staff when we meet up about once a year.

When I was in London on the MA course and looking round a bookshop, I spotted a small paperback with guidance for primary school head teachers. At the front there was this ancient Taoist poem:

Go with the people,
Live among them,
Learn from them,
Love them,
Start with what they know,
Build on what they have.
Of the best leaders
When their task is accomplished,
Their work done,
The people will remark,
'We have done it ourselves'.

Yes, that was what I believed about headship and was aiming to put into practice. Course leaders in the local authority asked me to speak on a couple of occasions about being a new head teacher and I gave this poem to my slightly newer colleagues. I hoped it focussed them on the role of a head teacher as it had me.

I was also asked to contribute to training for heads on health and safety, as I had attended a three-day intensive course on the subject. My knowledge came in very handy when we were having some modifications to the school building to allow wheelchair access to the hall and dining area. I was sitting in my office working as the builders were making a hole in our dining area wall to create space for a door. The taste and smell of the brick dust was wafting through to me. I decided to investigate. Sure enough, they had no dustsheets around where they were working to prevent the spread of particles to other areas of the school. I tackled the foreman, quoting the COSSH regulations I had learnt about on the course. The dustsheets soon appeared!

Some children in the school had entered an art competition sponsored by BT, and won. There were art material prizes for the children and a computer for the school. Neither my secretary nor I were able to operate effectively what was obviously an ex-BT computer and not at all suitable for use in a school. However, the children had been asked if they would like a character from their winning picture to visit the school. They chose one of the Red Indians they had drawn and a few months later we had news of a visit from a Red Indian circus act. The performer arrived to great excitement and was introduced to the winners. He was ready and very willing to perform his tricks with knives, axes and bows and arrows in the hall in front of the assembled school. A brief demonstration convinced me that he was a very skilled artist and he assured me that there would be no danger to the children. He didn't mention the staff! He persuaded two male staff to let him throw axes as they stood in front of a large wooden board. That went well. Then he fixed a balloon to the board and I knelt in front of it. He went to the back of the hall with his bow and arrow and a blindfold. He put on the blindfold and shot the arrow successfully at the balloon above my head. I will never forget the anxious look on the face of the small child sat in front of me as I waited for the arrow to hit its target. The assembled school broke into loud cheering and clapping. Well, I thought, that's one more thing to add to my job description! When, some months later, I was describing this event to the assistant director of education for Barnet, he was quite taken aback that I had taken such a risk, but then he had never been a head teacher.

The families we served were very appreciative of the work that the school did with their children and the care we showed towards them. Even though they visited us frequently, some infant children found the transfer to the juniors difficult. One boy in particular found the separation from his mother for a second time very traumatic. He was physically sick every morn-ing on the way to school and she was at the end of her tether. A wise infant school dinner lady brought them to me and we talked about the problem with him. I suggested that he had a star card on which I would put a gold star every day he came to school without being ill. We used this strategy for three weeks and it worked. The sickness stopped and he was settled happily in the juniors. His mother was so grateful and remembered me with an invitation several years later to his Bar Mitzvah. I was delighted when I also heard that he had taken leading roles in drama productions at his secondary school. This was one of the very few times I was privileged to know how a child in my care had developed into a confident adult. At Christmas and the end of each school year I was showered with gifts of appreciation from children and parents, an experience new to me in teaching.

In the school holidays my friends Cynthia and Brian and I had been staying in the Cotswolds with a view to retiring there when the time came. We bought a caravan and left it permanently on a camping site near Cirencester so that we could take short breaks at various times of the year. Circumstances, however, overtook us and we decided to move to the area sooner rather than later. Brian and Cynthia took over a village stores and post office and I started to look for headships in the same area. At my third interview I secured a headship of another junior school, this time in Tewkesbury. I had told my staff and governors that this was my intention, so it did not come as a surprise when I handed in my resignation. I set about making sure everything was in order for my successor whilst maintaining a good relationship with the chair of governors, who was not happy about my departure.

In the light of all that had happened while I had been the head of the school, I really wanted to say something that my staff would remember at my farewell speech. It was important to me that they realised the significance of their role in the life of their pupils, so I talked about my primary school teachers and the influence they had had on me to illustrate my point. As with many situations in teaching, it was impossible to gauge the outcome of my words, but they had to be said. I left Edgware on the Friday of the May bank holiday weekend in 1993 and began as a head teacher in Tewkesbury the following Tuesday.

Chapter Nine
My Second Headship

THE DAY I ARRIVED at my new job I was told that the school crossing patrol lady had died at the weekend and that her two daughters were members of the school. I had to lead my first assembly with a school I did not know and staff I had only just met and sensitively tell them this news. What a start! Fortunately, one of the more senior staff gave me some background information, which helped me deal appropriately with the situation.

At my appointment interview it was inferred that there were some difficult members of staff at the school. My previous experiences had led me to believe that I could cope with a situation of this kind and so I approached my new job with enthusiasm and fresh energy. Once again, the deputy head of the school had applied for the job of head teacher and been unsuccessful and so his cooperation and support had to be won. The advertisement for the job had said that the school would be expanding to a three-form entry school, which was what I had managed in Edgware, and the challenge of being involved with this expansion had attracted me to the post. In the event, this did not happen, but plenty of other challenges came my way.

My first term at the school was very much a familiarisation exercise. The building was only thirteen years old and required good maintenance rather than any major work. The standard of teaching was variable and my weekly check through staff planning and evaluation gave me the opportunity to make comments and suggestions. Training for teaching the National Curriculum had begun to improve and the introduction of the National Literacy and Numeracy Strategies was imminent. During that term I appointed a newly qualified teacher whose skills were in English and who later became an effective literacy coordinator.

The opportunity arose for me to complete an 'industrial placement' in a discipline of my own choice. I was determined that my new staff would be fully informed about child protection, so I approached the local social services and the NSPCC for placements with them in order to see how they tackled this area of their work, and as a result to write a policy for the school. I was successful, though in the event the NSPCC was able to be more helpful than social services. I tried hard to secure greater liaison with social services but they were only willing to take referrals from schools. They would not contact schools with information voluntarily. At various times I had children in the school about whom the staff and I had concerns regarding physical abuse and I referred them to social services. Sadly, they did not pursue my concerns for one particular family about which horrific details came to light in later years when the children were secure enough as adults and had the support they needed to disclose their childhood torture. When I read the account in the newspaper, I wished I had 'made a nuisance' of myself far more than I did on behalf of those children. Unless I enquired I was never told the outcome of social services' involvement or actions regarding children I referred to them.

The music teacher had heard me singing in assembly and asked me if I would take a small part in the school shows. I sang solos at the end of some productions for a while, but later opted out so that the focus would remain on the children. The local secondary school head attended one performance where I sang; he saw me step forward, expecting me to do the thank-you speech, and was utterly amazed when I began to sing! At least that's what he told me afterwards.

One important spin-off from the introduction of the National Curriculum was a tightening up of the requirements for collective worship. We were asked to ensure at least 51% of the content of our worship was Christian. Each week we had a visit from a local priest or minister to lead worship and, as a practising Christian myself, the worship I led was always based in Christian values and principles. One half term I decided to serialise *Pilgrim's Progress* in worship using a children's version of the story as my text. The children were captivated by the story and the names of Bunyan's characters fascinated and interested them. Class assemblies gradually became more values based and the children responded wholeheartedly to giving support to local charities with a link to the school. We fund-raised for Guide Dogs for the Blind when one of our parents was a puppy walker for the charity and for Angelman Syndrome when a pupil's sibling had been diagnosed with this condition.

I had been at the school for nearly two years when I reached my half-century. The staff made my day a very happy one and the cook provided my favourite pudding of lemon meringue pie. I had gifts from both teaching and support staff. From the support staff I had a flight in a glider. I waited until later in the year and at the summer half-term break booked my trip. I was very nervous but had the utmost faith in the pilot sat behind me in the plane. It was so amazing to sit in the cockpit looking down at the roads and fields beneath and only hearing the sound of the wind on the wings. It was an experience I will never forget.

Grant Maintained status was made available to schools by the government of the time. This meant that all the funds allocated to the school were managed by the head teacher and governors and there were no funds held by the Local Education Authority. I convinced my staff, governors and parents that this was the right step to take in order to retain for as long as possible the eight classes we had and to improve the provision within the school. The chair of governors who had appointed me felt he should resign over this issue due to his political affiliations. The new chairman was eager to take an active part in the life of the school and visited classes every Friday afternoon. I later discovered that as well as disrupting the last lessons of the week, he was also checking up on me behind my back. Staff asked me to curtail his visits and he reluctantly agreed.

In Gloucestershire, regular head teachers' meetings were held and sometimes there were outside speakers to add variety to the proceedings. One such speaker was from the government quango Investors in People. He claimed that undertaking the assessment for Investors in People would effectively prepare a school for the soon to be introduced Ofsted inspections. This caught my interest and so the school embarked on the process.

What I Did Since I Woke Up This Morning

We eventually gained the award once I had convinced the staff of its value and benefits. Our advisor for the award asked me once if the school was a church school. I'd like to think he picked up a Christian atmosphere in the school. What he did say was that he was impressed with the murals in the corridors which each year group had produced for the Millennium and which depicted significant times in the life of Jesus Christ.

I had attended management and appraisal training courses during my first headship and this continued with a serving headship course while I was in Tewkesbury. For this course I had to ask two teachers to complete a questionnaire about my leadership which I was not allowed to see, but the feedback was included as part of the course. On the last afternoon we had individual feedback on our performance on the course and from the questionnaires. I was devastated by what I heard. I had been led to believe that I was at least a good enough head teacher by my local authority advisor, but this was not what I was being told. I could not understand what I was hearing. I returned home feeling very broken and upset. I saw my advisor who reassured me that the findings were not a reflection of my capabilities as a head teacher but an inability on the part of the teachers to accept my ideas about change and improvement. It was not long after that when, in a staff meeting, I challenged any staff who might not agree with my style of leadership to look elsewhere for a job. No one put in any applications that year and some showed me greater respect.

My deputy head decided to take early retirement and, for financial reasons, could not be replaced. Two senior staff were appointed but were ineffective in their roles, providing me with more problems than support. Added to that, the new secretary, who had presented with such great potential, began to adopt a negative attitude and become very uncooperative. Fortunately for me, my clerical assistant had a super sense of humour and could see what I was trying to achieve in the school. She helped keep me afloat in what was a very difficult period of my headship. Likewise, the local head teachers' group, where I was able to talk through the difficulties I was experiencing with one or two of my fellow heads. Of course, my family unwaveringly supported me. Sadly, we had a family bereavement around the time of these difficulties and I was knocked for six. I had some time off at the end of the school year to recover and returned the next term. In the meantime, I met with governors who were unsympathetic and continued to be critical. Union support was not at all positive and so, once again, with family support I had to grow through this experience myself.

The light at the end of the tunnel began to get brighter when the Government introduced early retirement for teachers and two more of my staff decided to take the opportunity to go. I was then able to appoint two young and enthusiastic newly qualified teachers who brought the energy and freshness that the school badly needed. One of them was a music specialist whose ability far outstripped that of his predecessor. The children sang their hearts out for him and together he and the other new teacher put on several really good shows, her contribution being the direction and organisation of each production. As usual, I dealt with 'front of house' and made several costumes and some props. One afternoon after the children had gone home I wandered out into the hall to see why there was the sound of laughter and happy adult voices drifting towards my room. I found several of the younger members of staff busily engaged, brushes and palettes in hand, in painting the Yellow Brick Road on our stage for the imminent performance of *The Wizard of Oz*. These were really happy times when the school felt united and criticisms were set aside. Once again, the healing and uniting influence of laughter and music ringing round the school building brought smiles to people's faces.

The end of the spring term in school is often determined by the date of Easter, and usually April 1st falls in the Easter holiday. One year, however, we were in school on that day and the idea of playing an April Fool's joke on the whole school came up as the staff gathered for a before school chat and cup of coffee. It was suggested that we set the children a task which they would complete on the school field at playtime. We decided to tell them that a very rare plant had been discovered growing on our field and we had received a letter from an important research organisation asking us to search for this plant. The plant was given a Latin name which was an anagram of 'April Fool', and I drew a picture of it on an overhead transparency sheet. With appropriately serious expressions we went into assembly as usual. At the end of the worship I told the school about the letter, showed them the picture on the screen and asked them all to search our field at playtime and to come and tell me when they had found the plant. What I had drawn was Scarlet Pimpernel, a plant I knew was not native to our area but one I had seen on Scilly. Sure enough, they all went out and looked very diligently for the plant while we peeped through the classroom windows watching them. No one came to me to say that they had found the plant, but one year six child did unscramble the anagram. I asked him to keep it to himself. We called the whole school into the hall just after twelve noon and 'April Fooled' them. The ruse had worked and we had really enjoyed ourselves. We were threatened with 'getting you back next year', but next year we would conveniently not be in school on April 1st!

I had introduced a reward system to the school and talked with the children about what were appropriate prizes for specific numbers of house points. Children were sent to me for their rewards and I recorded them in a special file which was kept in the entrance hall. A new child was being shown around the school by an older pupil one day and I overheard him telling the visitor about the awards file with great pride and enthusiasm. It felt good to realise how important this was in the life of the school. There was also a system of blue and yellow slips which told me about either an exceptional piece of work or behaviour, or the reverse. In both cases, parents were informed about their children's successes and misdemeanours. The system worked well.

The day came when my secretary brought in the 'brown envelope' from Ofsted. We had a year's notice for our inspection and it gave us, what I can now see with hindsight, too much time to think and prepare. I had a new chair of governors who was the local rector based at the parish church in our area. She was a great support to me and her faith and belief in me had helped to dispel the demons of earlier experiences. The Ofsted inspection reflected well the standards the school had achieved, as did our SATs results, which were regularly above the county average.

To celebrate the end of the inspection our music teacher had organised a visit to a theatre in Bristol to see *Les Miserables*. It was a fantastic production and we all had a great evening out together with partners and friends. The next day I was told by the year six teacher that she had found a poison pen letter in her bag of marking the previous evening from what appeared to be members of her class. Later that same morning another letter was found addressed to a year three teacher and the computer font was identical. Whatever I had planned to do that day was put on hold. An investigation had to take place. I interviewed groups and individuals from the year six class and got nowhere. I discussed the situation with the class teacher. I decided finally to hold an assembly and speak to the whole school about it and say that I would involve the police if no one could give me any information. This brought about a confession from one of the three boys responsible and the names of the other two.

The two staff were deeply offended by the letters; one contained threatening remarks about her children and the other made personal comments about the teacher's appearance. Both of them were very upset. I saw it as my duty to protect and defend my staff. I initially temporarily excluded the three boys whilst I approached the situation in a rational manner. I sought advice from the local authority, but this was not forthcoming to any great extent because we were a Grant Maintained school. I then permanently excluded the boys and this prompted an appeal by the parents. The appeal was heard by the appeals committee of the governing body with, at last, some advice from the local authority. For this appeal I had gathered my evidence of the events as they happened and the teachers' feelings about the offensiveness of the letters. The appeal was upheld because I had not consulted sufficiently with the parents due to lack of advice from the authority. However, the governors would only reinstate the boys if the parents would agree to them seeing an educational psychologist. They refused to do this and so the boys were found places in other local schools, to the relief of the year six teacher, who never wanted to see them in her class again.

In Tewkesbury there is a magnificent abbey where worship has taken place for many hundreds of years. Using the abbey for a year six leavers' service evolved as an idea on a religious education course I attended with one of my teachers. I took the suggestion to the local head teachers' meeting and it was warmly received. I felt we needed a banner of some kind to represent the Tewkesbury Primary Schools which could be displayed at the service. It took rather more effort to get this agreed, but when I offered to organise the making and finishing of the banner myself it got the stamp of approval. Each school had a quarter metre square of fabric to decorate on both sides. One side was to be symbols of a curriculum subject and the other side the school badge. I provided the fabrics and the instructions and waited. One by one the squares were returned to me completed and I sewed them together, made loops for a T-bar on which the banner would hang and sewed a fringe round the edge. Each school contributed towards the cost of the materials and a friend made the T-bar and pole needed to carry the banner into the abbey. Meanwhile, each school was preparing an item for the service. The first leavers' service in the abbey was a really meaningful experience for all of us and it has continued as a tradition ever since. It will long be a very special memory for me.

What I Did Since I Woke Up This Morning

Liaison with the infant school strengthened to some extent during my headship. We shared an afternoon picnic and entertainment to celebrate the Queen's Golden Jubilee and I visited the school prior to the children transferring to us. Our greatest joint venture was working on a bid for a grant to cover the cost of an ICT technician to be shared by five of the local schools. Our bid was successful and all the schools, which by now had computer suites, were able to benefit from his skills.

We accepted students from Gloucestershire College of Higher Education on their teaching placements for some of the time that I was at the school and I made some very useful contacts through this professional dialogue. The tutor allocated to one student came to speak with me one day about the constant negative feedback her student was getting from his class teacher. I addressed the issue with the teacher, who felt affronted by this and asked for a meeting with her union representative and the college tutor. The matter was resolved but not before it had become a mountain rather than a molehill.

Observations of teaching took place on a regular basis and were formally recorded and fed back to teachers. The local authority advisor occasionally observed lessons as well and we discussed the standard of teaching and how it could be improved. Governors were allocated to subjects and liaised with subject coordinators about visiting lessons so that they could report to governing body meetings. It was when I was observing an experienced year four teacher that I witnessed him hit a child's hand. I followed the disciplinary procedures for this and he did not repeat the behaviour, but when the time did eventually come that we had to make a teacher redundant, he offered to take it. His offer was accepted.

I managed the school without any senior staff or a deputy head for over a year before a vacancy provided the opportunity to advertise for a deputy head teacher. Finally, the governors agreed to allocate the funds needed to employ a deputy head and it was with great anticipation that I waited to see what applications would arrive in the post. The person appointed was absolutely right for the job. Coming from another junior school, he was able to make realistic comparisons of what we were achieving and was extremely complimentary. We built a good working relationship and his support was a great boost to my confidence, particularly as initiatives were still coming from central government thick and fast, the latest of these being the introduction of performance management for head teachers.

It was after a meeting with the governors' sub-committee assigned the task of evaluating my performance and setting my next year's targets that I began to wonder what more could be asked of me. I was old enough by now to take early retirement and gave the idea considerable thought. I made all the necessary enquiries about finance and then made my decision to retire. My family were in full support of my decision. My deputy head was rather taken aback and the chair of governors was disappointed but understanding. I contacted the people I knew at Gloucestershire College of Higher Education about working as a link tutor and offered my services as an acting head teacher to the local authority. I let local schools know I would be available for supply teaching. Why did I do all this? I knew I needed a rest but I also knew I could never be totally idle, and, of course, the money would come in handy.

What I Did Since I Woke Up This Morning

Again I wondered what I should say in my leaving speech. I mulled over a few ideas and then thought it would be best to summarise my career and what it meant to me. For many reasons I could not refer to certain members of staff who had been hard working and supportive without making those I was not mentioning blatantly obvious. General terminology seemed the best solution. But there was something special I did want to do. Throughout my life and my career, music had been really important to me. I had introduced to the school a talented pianist who played for shows when there was no music teacher and who taught children to play the piano. He came along to my retirement party as a member of staff, but at a given moment at the end of my speech he went to the piano. I was going out on a song! I sang the verses of Abba's 'Thank you for the music' and asked everyone to join in the chorus. It expressed in the best way I knew everything I felt. It was time to move on.

Chapter Ten
Using my Skills

MY RETIREMENT COINCIDED WITH my friends Cynthia and Brian's ruby wedding anniversary and we invited friends and relatives to our joint party. It was a very happy occasion and was followed by a wonderful final assembly at school where year six said their goodbyes to the school and to me. They even sang a

Teaching

special song for me from the film *Billy Elliot*, and in true 'Annie' style chorused 'We love you, Miss Hammant'! It needed great self-control to smile without the tears!

The next day we left for our annual holiday on the Isles of Scilly, and for the first time we were not camping. Cynthia had had two knee joints replaced and was not able to cope with camping that year. We stayed in bed and breakfast accommodation on the same island as always, Bryher. The weather was glorious and I enjoyed rest and relaxation in the sun with no need to think or plan for school in September.

I did some supply teaching at local schools and began working as a link tutor for Gloucestershire College of Higher Education in that first year of my retirement. The skills I had developed from my early days teaching in Sunday school through to those of headship continued to be of value to me. The following summer I was contacted about taking on an acting headship in a Church of England village primary school and began in the September. The head teacher had decided to return to being a class teacher and had tendered his resignation. I was to lead the school during the time it took the governors to replace him. I accepted the role on a part-time basis of four days a week, leaving space to continue my work for the university. I enjoyed enormously meeting other teachers and working in a primary school. I stayed for two terms. There was an Ofsted inspection a month before I left when the school was deemed to be satisfactory. The report included remarks about the excellent leadership of the acting head teacher. I had taught the year six booster classes and was observed by an inspector for a literacy lesson when we studied poetry. I chose the poem 'Warning' by Jenny Joseph, to which the children responded very well, especially when they noticed the first line read 'When I am an old woman I shall wear purple' and I was wearing a purple outfit!

During the inspection one particular infant child made his mark on the event. Dion and his sister were foster children. They had only been in the school a few months and had to travel to school in minibus transport from a nearby town. Despite having had breakfast, Dion would always eat his break time snack on the bus instead of saving it for the right time in school. Previous experience had taught him to eat any food he was given straight away as there was very little of it. The escort on the bus tried to persuade him not to do this, but generally failed. It was the last day of the inspection and we were surviving on the chocolates given to us by the chair of governors. The special needs teacher was passing the staffroom door, which was situated near the infant classroom, when she saw Dion come out of the staffroom with a face smeared with chocolate. She asked him if he had eaten chocolates from the tin in the staffroom and he denied it. She said she could smell chocolate on his breath and see sweet papers on the floor, but he still denied it. She spoke to his class teacher, who sent him to me with a note on a yellow slip. Eventually, he admitted what he had done. We thought the matter was closed, but the next day a similar thing happened with food from his sister's bag. On the third day, which was a Friday, the letter about his behaviour which he had been given to take home to his foster parents was found in a toilet pan. This gave me considerable cause for concern and I realised that normal sanctions were not enough for this little boy. He needed help. Over the weekend I decided to use a star card with him and talked to him about it on the Monday morning. Each day when he ate his snack at the right time he would get a gold star. Three stars in a row would give him a small chocolate bar. The system worked beautifully for the four weeks left of the term, during which time I increased the number of stars required for a chocolate bar to four. I passed on the details of the strategy to the new head teacher, who later told me it had continued to work well until it was no longer needed.

During the first week of the summer term I was again contacted by the local authority about another school needing an acting head teacher. This time the head teacher had suddenly become ill within a week of an Ofsted inspection. I was asked to manage this situation and in particular support the staff, who were feeling totally abandoned. This was a village Church of England school with just two classes. The infant class had one teacher and a teaching assistant, but the junior class had two part-time teachers plus the head teacher. One of these ladies took on his teaching role so that I was able to focus on assisting the inspectors as much as possible and try to keep morale high. A problem arose with the chair of governors, who had been in to school to try to help before I arrived. Even though telephone messages had been left for him, he arrived on my first morning completely unaware of my existence and was very rude to me. In the circumstances, I ignored this and listened to his life history and opinions about education until he calmed down. I assured him I would keep him informed of events as they developed.

The inspectors were thorough and very professional in sharing their findings with me, knowing that I had no influence over what had been happening in the school as far as the children's education was concerned. The school was placed into special measures, to the utter amazement of some of the governors. The staff were shaken but determined to get back on track. It was the parents who were most perplexed and wanting answers to their concerns. I listened to their worries before and after the outcome of the inspection was made public and gave as much reassurance and information as was appropriate. As a result of pressure from his fellow governors, the chairman resigned and then the journey towards a better future for the school began. Before the end of my term at the school another acting head teacher had been appointed to lead the school as it worked its way out of special measures. Local authority training to address the improvements needed in teaching had also started.

The school was a church school and the local vicar was the vice chair of governors. His efforts to bring a Christian influence into the school had been thwarted by the negative attitude of the head teacher towards worship. A daily act of worship had not been taking place for some time. I immediately changed this and we held collective worship regularly. I had a very special book called *The Woodland Gospels* by Jeremy Lloyd, which told the story of the life of Christ. It was perfect for these children. It had characters in it they could identify with, and it gave expression to a range of feelings as the story unfolded. The whole age range found it entertaining and easy to understand. They loved it. By the time the church inspection arrived some weeks after the Ofsted inspection, the school was functioning more effectively as a church school and was deemed satisfactory.

Whilst I was in my first acting headship I had been approached by the Diocesan Director of Education to train as a church school inspector. I decided this would be something I could do as a retired head teacher and duly applied to go on a course to train. Courses were held twice a year and I opted for one in January 2005, which was held over three days in a hotel. It was interesting to meet other prospective inspectors and work through the requirements for what were then Section 23 inspections. I passed the final test paper, which we completed in our hotel rooms, with flying colours and was set to begin my inspection role. Since then a more rigorous approach to church school inspections has been introduced and regular training takes place to maintain high standards.

My last acting headship was at another village Church of England school where the head teacher was seriously ill but receiving treatment. She had not decided to take early retirement at this point and we met fairly regularly to chat and for me to keep her up to date with events at her school. I was the third acting head teacher during her illness and soon became aware how hard the staff and governors had worked to keep the school functioning effectively in her absence. A period of stability was badly needed. Part of my role was to teach the mixed year five and six class for two days a week. It was wonderful being back in the classroom and we had a really great time learning together, the class and I, particularly on Friday afternoon games lessons. Luckily for me, the children knew the rules of football. I knew about the importance of having fun and plenty of exercise and so between us we achieved a very happy ending to the week. Another bonus was that the church was located right next door to the school and we held worship there every day. I had my first experience of 'Open the Book' at this school and was very impressed with the way the team told Bible stories to the children and involved them in the action. When an appeal was made for more members of a similar team at my own church, I joined and have loved being part of telling those stories ever since.

One very tragic event took place while I was the acting head. The father of one of the boys in my class committed suicide. We needed to deal with this situation sensitively and with the appropriate background knowledge. I contacted Winston's Wish and we received extremely helpful advice and support from a member of their team. The chair of governors was the parish priest and he visited the family, giving support and comfort. The funeral was at the church next to the school one Saturday morning. The boy in my class asked if he could read prayers in the service and the priest agreed and was by his side to help if needed. He began, "Hands together and eyes closed," as was the tradition in the school, and then confidently read the prayer for his dad. Our class made him a card on which they had all written a personal message. I sent him the 'school bear' to look after him. His mother told me later that she often found him reading the card during the early days of their bereavement. He kept the bear.

I worked at the school for three terms in total. During that time the head teacher did decide to retire and sadly died a few years later. By that time a new head had been appointed and the school was in a position to move into the next stage of its development. This I am delighted to see when I visit students at the school as their link tutor.

My happiest moment at the school was a harvest thanksgiving service in the church when my class sang John Rutter's 'All things bright and beautiful' during the service. That I will never forget, as they sang it so beautifully and every single child was focussed and involved.

The four years since I completed my work as an acting head teacher have been filled with a variety of increasingly varied and interesting roles at the University of Gloucestershire, plus my inspection work. I was asked to work as an assessor for Early Years Professionals and to assess unqualified teachers who are working towards gaining qualified status. Teaching religious education, leading professional studies seminars and marking assignments have been interesting as well. In all these roles it has again become crystal clear what an important and significant role teachers play in the life of a child.

When I sit in lessons and listen and watch as students explain concepts and interact with children of all abilities, I witness some amazing happenings. I was in a year five lesson which had gone really well and at the end the student was challenging the children to set a target for themselves ready for the next lesson. Quite out of the blue a voice next to me said, "What is your target?" For a second I was taken aback, but then replied, "To make sure you are learning what your teacher is teaching you."

Particularly in infant classes I am often greeted with, "Hello, who are you?" Young children are so accepting and curious because their teacher has made school a happy and safe place for them. Sometimes I have even been welcomed with, "Hello, you're here again!"

I was watching a numeracy lesson one morning where the student was gradually filling a suitcase with all the things she would need to go on a holiday to Australia and asking children to test if it was heavier or lighter as she filled it. On completion of this task, she picked up the case ready to leave for her holiday when a little voice was heard to say, "You can't go. You are supposed to be teaching us!" How must that student have felt about her importance to those children as she thought about this afterwards? This is the role and responsibility of all teachers.

I was sitting in the entrance hall of a school one day waiting for a teacher to return a computer disc when a small boy came past. I don't know if he thought that I was in some kind of trouble or difficulty, but he paused and came over to me and put his arm round my shoulder in a hug-like gesture. He smiled but said nothing. I said, "Thank you; that was so nice of you," and he went on his way. I was really moved by his kindness and marvelled at his open, caring nature, which had clearly been nurtured by all the influences on his young life, including his school.

The Association of Christian Teachers has a prayer which teachers can use as they consider the importance and significance of the role they share with Our Lord. It says this:

> *Lord our God, we thank you that you made each one of us in your image and likeness, and that we are all your beloved children.*
>
> *We pray for the children/students we teach.*
>
> *We pray for students/children who make us smile, test our patience, we find easy to like, are bright, are hardworking, get on our nerves, like to laugh, always look lost, never say a word, remind us of ourselves when we were younger, challenge our way of thinking, we find difficult to like, find learn-*

*ing tough, are a delight, always look sad, talk all
the time, are easily overlooked, are impossible to
ignore.*

*We thank you for all students/children who have an
impact on our lives and for the privilege of having
an impact on their lives.*

*Lord, help us not to label those we teach or to fall into
the trap of thinking we have got them sussed. Help
us to be open to new revelations and the work of
your Holy Spirit in each of their lives.*

*Lord, use those we teach to teach us. Help us to be
Christ-like at all times, seeing each one with your
eyes and valuing them with your heart of love.*

We ask this prayer in the name of Jesus the teacher.

Amen

The joy of working at the university has been the respect which has been shown towards me as a person and the acknowledgement of my skills and experience as a head teacher by both staff and students. It has affirmed to me that I have been able to demonstrate throughout my career that Mary Salter's assessment of my potential to be a successful teacher was right. I also believe that God has used me to touch the lives of others through my work in education. I have a fridge magnet which reads 'Teaching is a work of heart', and it truly is! At times it can almost break your heart, and at other times it can fill your heart with immeasurable joy.